The so-called Fourth Industrial Revolution has prompted companies to adapt to a new business paradigm based on digital interconnection and the ability to respond quickly to the needs of consumers and users.

These conditions are closely related to the advent of digital technologies that enable the real-time integration of devices and the control of production systems through technological platforms.

Based on this logic, this volume aims to investigate the forms and methods being used by the company at present to confront the new business paradigm, commonly known as Industry 4.0, as well as the impact of new digital technologies on corporate evolutionary dynamics and related business models. More specifically, technological challenges will assess the impact of new technologies on productivity and investment in complementary resources—including human, organizational, and managerial capital—as well as the effects related to the introduction of Internet of Things (IoT)-based production processes.

By following this approach, the focus subsequently shifts to drone technology, which is considered by many to be one of the most revolutionary Industry 4.0 technologies. In addition to investigating the history and potential applications of drones, many of which proved to be fundamental during the COVID-19 pandemic, the volume emphasizes the related ethical and social aspects such as the degree of knowledge regarding and the public acceptance of drones. The academic and professional approach of this volume allows it to serve as a guide for professionals, entrepreneurs, and academics with a particular interest in both digital innovation and the drone sector.

Bernardino Quattrociocchi is Full Professor of Management at the Sapienza University of Rome's Faculty of Economics.

Mario Calabrese, PhD, is Associate Professor of Management, Department of Management, Sapienza University of Rome.

Francesca Iandolo, PhD, is Tenure-track Lecturer in Management, Department of Management, Sapienza University of Rome.

Francesco Mercuri, PhD, is Adjunct Professor in Production Management and Logistic Systems, the Department of Management, the Faculty of Economics, the Sapienza University of Rome.

T0347949

Industry Dynamics and Industry 4.0
Drones for Remote Sensing Applications

Bernardino Quattrociocchi, Mario Calabrese,
Francesca Iandolo, Francesco Mercuri

Industry Dynamics
and Industry 4.0

Drones for Remote Sensing Applications

 G. Giappichelli Editore

First published 2023
by Routledge
4 Park Square, Milton Park, Abingdon, Oxon OX14 4RN

and by Routledge
605 Third Avenue, New York, NY 10158

Routledge is an imprint of the Taylor & Francis Group, an informa business

and by G. Giappichelli Editore
Via Po 21, Torino – Italia

British Library Cataloguing-in-Publication Data
A catalogue record for this book is available from the British Library

Library of Congress Cataloging-in-Publication Data
A catalogue record for this book has been requested

ISBN: 978-1-032-35861-1 (hbk-Routledge)
ISBN: 978-1-003-32904-6 (ebk-Routledge)
ISBN: 978-1-032-35864-2 (pbk-Routledge)
ISBN: 978-88-921-4251-0 (hbk-Giappichelli)

Typeset in Simoncini Garamond
by G. Giappichelli Editore, Turin, Italy

The manuscript has been subjected to a peer review process prior to publication.

Publication carried out as part of the R&D project "SPS DEHTEC - Development & Hybrid Testing Center, funded on the Call referred to in the General Regulation of the exempted aid schemes n.17 of 30 September 2014 - Title II Chapter 2 (Aid to integrated programs promoted by PMI) Notice for the submission of projects promoted by small businesses".

Contents

Acknowledgments

This volume is the result of a course of study and research on Industry 4.0. In the present research, particular attention was paid to the tools and applications in support of corporate digital transformation. In this context, the R&D project, "SPS DEHTEC – Development & Hybrid Testing Center" has been developed and financed by the Structural Funds of Puglia Region. I would like to sincerely thank all the institutions and research organizations that supported this project for their commitment and dedication. In particular, I wish to thank the Prometeo S.r.l., a project partner, as well as Gianluca Cecchet, Massimo Di Fazio, Davide D'Arcangelo, Paolo Bianchi and Emanuela Persico, without whom the project could not have been completed.

I would like to extend a special thanks to the "MOF–Centro Agroalimentare di Fondi" and to its members (Lazio Region, Euromof Consortium, Municipality of Fondi, Frosinone, and Latina Chamber of Commerce, Banca Popolare di Fondi, and Banca Unicredit), to the administrator Enzo Addessi, and to all the operators who gave me the opportunity to increase my experience and knowledge with respect to the agri-food chain-one of the most complex and important sectors at the international level.

I also want to extend my special thanks to Salvatore De Meo, Member of the European Parliament, for providing me with a European framework and important input on the topics discussed.

In addition, I would like to thank the company Sinergica s.r.l. for having believed and supported-even economically-the project idea behind this editorial work.

Moreover, I would like to express my gratitude to my friends Fabio Benvenuti and Vincenzo Contri for cooperating with me in managing the editorial project.

Finally, my gratitude goes out to all the colleagues and authors involved in the creation of this volume, Mario Calabrese, Francesca Iandolo, and Francesco Mercuri-as well as to the Department of Management of the University of Rome, Sapienza, for having always stimulated and encouraged our academic research activities.

With great affection,
Bernardino Quattrociocchi, Sapienza, University of Rome, July 2021

Preface

The Fourth Industrial Revolution has encouraged companies to adapt to a new business paradigm based on digital interconnection and the ability to respond increasingly quickly to the needs of consumers and users. This has been further amplified in recent years, in which the spread of COVID-19 has conclusively highlighted how digital innovation and the rethinking of business models should be considered increasingly crucial factors for business survival in the present era. These are conditions that are closely related to the advent of new digital technologies, which enable the real-time integration of devices and systems for production control through technological platforms.

In this context, drones and robots play a notable role. Drones, indeed, comprise an integral part of this process; owing to their physical and technological characteristics, drones can be used in different industrial sectors (military, security, energy, transport, agriculture, etc.), and their potential can be exploited even in areas that are not accessible to humans.

Given this logic, the present Volume aims to investigate the forms and methods with which the company is now facing the new business paradigm, commonly known as Industry 4.0 (Pedrazzini, 2018) as well as the impact of new digital technologies on the evolutionary dynamics of the company and related business models. More specifically, the Volume proposes an assessment of the impact of new technologies on productivity and investment in complementary resources–such as human, organizational, and managerial capital–as well as the effects on production processes related to the introduction of the Internet of Things (IoT).

When following this approach, the focus is subsequently shifted to drone technology, which is considered by many to be one of the revolutionary technologies in the context of Industry 4.0; in addition to investigating its history and potential applications, many of which proved to be fundamental during the COVID-19 pandemic, the Volume also emphasizes the ethical and social aspects of drones, such as the degree of knowledge and public acceptance regarding them.

The Volume, which was drawn up through an academic and professional approach, is proposed as a manual for professionals, entrepreneurs, and academics with a particular interest both in digital innovation and the sector of drones.

Finally, following these brief introductory notes, our dutiful and sincere thanks go to those colleagues who, with their skills and their passion, have contributed to our professional growth.

Fabio Massimo Castaldo – Vice-President of the European Parliament, July 2021

Introduction

Technological innovation related to Industry 4.0 has revolutionized the manufacturing industry. The most interesting and challenging aspect of this revolution concerns the optimization of numerous aspects of the organizational structure of a company. Digital transformation, which has a profound impact on the entire value chain, is an essential element for determining a company's competitive advantage. This new production paradigm aims to make the organization of work and the methods of production more efficient; however, a new system configuration will be required to improve the relations between the company and its stakeholders as well as internal and external communication.

Precisely because of the substantial magnitude of the consequences of this innovative scenario–the reorganization of the structure and of the production activities of the company–the process in progress has been identified as the "Fourth Industrial Revolution," also known as "Industry 4.0" in the literature.

The transition from the Third Industrial Revolution, which encapsulates the latter half of the 20th century, to the fourth was driven by the transition from analog equipment to those based on digital technologies owing to the rapid development of information technology (IT) or information and communication technology (ICT), which is characterized by the convergence of computer science and electronics. Major societal changes followed this transition and, in many ways, still serve as harbingers of further developments. In this new dimension, technologies such as Big Data, cloud computing, advanced robotics, and artificial intelligence (AI) have resulted in the new production paradigm called "Industry 4.0" (Pedrazzini, 2018). This paradigm provides an organizational method for the production of goods and services that is based, first and foremost, on the integration of physical systems, plants, and machinery with digital technologies through an efficient connection to a network that enables the collection and analysis of information for the improvement of the production cycle. In addition, the widespread use of the IoT, wherein electronic devices in a network are embedded with software that allows it to exchange data with other connected devices, also promotes the development of the Fourth Industrial Revolution.

The term "Industry 4.0" has its genesis in the German expression "Industrie 4.0" (and the subsequent English "Industry 4.0"), which was derived from a specific research document entitled "Zukunftsprojekt Industrie 4.0" that is, "Project for the Industry of the Future 4.0." The aforementioned study was presented at the 2011 Hannover Fair as part of the German government's broader *High-Tech Strategy 2020 Action Plan* for the digitization of production processes and products themselves.

Consequently, this new paradigm based on innovation completely changes a company's approach to both production and market, forcing it to change the structural references and even to seek new professionalism and skills. The perception of value itself and corporate strategies also change with the technologies that drive the new scenario considered herein.

This publication describes the forms and methods with which a company is tasked with developing a new business model that is capable of governing the transformation of said company and serving as a tool for aligning technological development and the creation of economic value. The term "business model" refers to "an architecture of products, services, and information flows" (Timmers, 1998), thus configuring an abstract, exemplary description of business activity. The perspective chosen by the present publication aims to assess the impact of new technologies on productivity and investments in complementary resources, such as human, organizational, and managerial capital, as well as the impact of IoT on production processes, which allows for an increasing amount of information to be made available throughout the value chain. From the latter perspective, companies are called to address various challenges, such as privacy and security measures for protecting the data generated by the IoT, given that its use in business processes significantly affects not only the quality and range of products, up to their extreme personalization, but also the dialogic dynamics with the market and with all the target audiences in a continuous circuit that consists of information exchanges in real time. The transition to Industry 4.0, therefore, affects every aspect of the structure of a company, beginning with the same business models and extending to the logistics systems.

Consequently, changing the production paradigm, or moving to Business 4.0, entails managing machines, products, and human resources in an integrated and intelligent manner.

Among the various enabling technologies that characterize the ongoing innovative process in many respects, some are destined to have a decisive impact on the transformation of business processes. These technologies include the use of clouds and augmented reality vision systems, the interconnection of tools and machinery by means of the development of internet networks, Big Data analytics, and cyber security, among others.

Support for 5G technology, which allows for faster and smarter networks, is a crucial factor in grafting these technologies into business processes. These new technologies will have a profound impact on the use and enhancement of data as well as on the level of human–machine interaction, thus opening a new chapter of skills and necessitating a requalification of labor resources.

As shown in the diagram below, the Gartner Hype Cycle for Emerging Technologies 2020 identifies 30 technology skill profiles that will have a significant impact on society and business in the next 5 to 10 years. The Gartner tool employs the unique hype cycles, which distill over 1,700 technologies into a list of must-know technologies and trends. The 2020 data highlights the following five unique trends:

- composite architectures,
- algorithmic trust,
- beyond silicon,
- training AI, and
- digital me.

Fig. A. Hype Cycle for Emerging Technologies, 2021

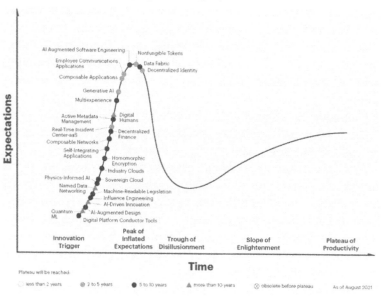

Source: www.gartner.it – https://www.gartner.com/smarterwithgartner/3-themes-surface-in-the-2021-hype-cycle-for-emerging-technologies.

The training AI, a type of AI that is capable of dynamically changing to respond to a situation, for example, adapting over time to technologies that are capable of generating new models to solve specific problems, is one of the most interesting pieces of evidence proposed by the Gartner data. This is the case with generative AI, which can create new content (images, videos, etc.) and alter existing content. The new artifacts are similar, but not identical, to the original ones.

The fifth trend examined by Gartner, called "digital me," comprises technologies that entail the creation of digital integration systems between man and technology. Bidirectional brain-machine interfaces, for example, are wearable devices that allow bidirectional communication between a human brain and a computer or machine interface. The potential applications of these devices include authentication, access and payment, immersive analytics, and exoskeletons in the field of business relationships.

Here, the timeline proposed by Gartner highlights the continuous evolution of technologies that can be applied to business processes and the related innovative skills and professional figures that might be required by the market; in addition, it suggests ideas for planning investments in IT. In a context such as that of the ever-changing Industry 4.0, there is a need for new professional figures such as digital business analysts, cyber security experts, hardware engineers, and architects of new technological and organizational systems.

Various government projects have been promoted and implemented in Europe to transfer the concept of Industry 4.0 to the entrepreneurial fabric and encourage the adoption and development of technologies related to the Fourth Industrial Revolution: "Industrie 4.0 in Germany, "Industrie du Futur" in France, Smart Industry" in the Netherlands, and "Catapult–High-Value Manufacturing" in the United Kingdom (UK) are all investment support and incentive activities with similar characteristics and objectives. These initiatives are all characterized by arrangements of tax incentives and financing for companies that intend to evolve according to digital connection and integration models. The system adopted by Italy that starts from the 2017 Budget Law, which is named "National Industry 4.0 Plan," ensures the financial commitment of the government in supporting tangible and intangible investments from a multi-year perspective. This regulatory system includes various incentive profiles, which primarily concern tax relief measures for plant and machinery as well as for research and development expenses. The Italian incentive system stimulates the creation of appropriate network infrastructures and the provision of public support tools to guarantee private investments and facilitate the transition toward the new production paradigm (Quattrociocchi, 2020).

As might be expected, even the boundaries of the technological world enclosed in Industry 4.0 are destined to be overcome, at least in the instrumental sphere if not in the regulatory one, by the evolution of innovation that begins to prefigure the lines of an "Industry 5.0" profile. This evolution can be seen in the introduction of collaborative robots or cobots, which can communicate with operators and improve their performance, into specific production processes with obvious benefits for the health and safety of workers as well as for the competitiveness of a company in terms of its environmental impact. In other words, such an evolution is the "Human Technology Oriented" model defined by the Japanese manufacturing world.

It is therefore essential to understand the consequences of technological innovation for the value chain of a company and for business models as well as how these consequences can generate the differences that determine a company's competitive advantage.

According to a 2018 Deloitte research (Report Italia 4.0, www. deloitte.com/it), Italian business executives are particularly aware that the implementation of new technologies is a key factor for competitive differentiation on the market, with 32% stating that they "completely agree" on this point. Consequently, Italian companies recognize the importance of adopting new 4.0 technologies to remain competitive in the future and have started investing in them.

One company function that is particularly involved in undergoing changes in in terms of its production processes is **logistics**, which will be considered here. It is interesting to confirm how technological innovations with numerous applications, such as blockchain, can have a significant impact in the field of external logistics. These systems enable the certification of information and transactions carried out between the network nodes, similar to a distributed public register. Indeed, I have already adopted numerous blockchain-based projects in various sectors, from financial to healthcare services as well as mobile payments, logistics, and supply chain management.

Among the various applications of 4.0 technologies, it seemed interesting to conduct an in-depth exploration of a product that offers unique insights regarding the services that can potentially be linked to it: **the drone**. This object is characterized by wide diffusion, particularly in areas that strictly concern the delivery phase of goods, especially in some parts of the world, as already implemented by the giant Amazon.

In any case, drones certainly constitute one of the most noteworthy technological innovations in recent years, particularly with respect to possible applications in multiple fields and so much so that the intervention of the technologies related to it now extend far beyond its use for hobby purposes—an initially preferential field of application–and move toward the diffusion of the drone at a general level.

The data on the trend of the sector evince some curious projections. As per the most recent analyses and as highlighted in the following figure, which was presented by the consulting firm Arthur D. Little at the Dronitaly in Milan (the most important Italian exhibition in the sector, with data from the latest publications from the firm, namely, from April 4 and 5, 2019), the global growth of the remote piloted systems market will reach significant figures by 2028, equal to a value of 25 billion US dollars and corresponding to approximately 19.3 million units sold.

Fig. B. Remotely Piloted Aircraft Systems' (RPASs) Market Evolution

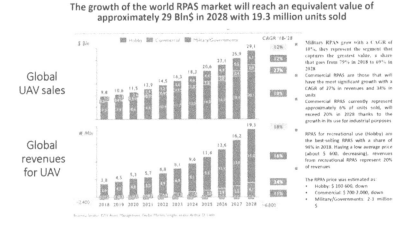

Source: Arthur D. Little (2019).

Crucially, the services sector linked to the use of drones will benefit from the rapid expansion of the market given the opening of new spaces and areas of application favored by continuous technological innovation, which will specifically involve cameras, sensory applications, and three-dimensional mapping. The global payload market will hit 7 billion dollars in 2022.

Of the applications that are being paid increasing attention is drone delivery, which has already been announced by the major players in the sector and, as in the case of DHL, has been launched in limited areas. The following figure illustrates how the commercial applications of remotely piloted aircraft systems (RPASs) will become more prevalent in various fields, with a clear impact on the business models of numerous services.

Fig. C. Main Fields of the Future Applications of RPAS Services

Applications
The RPAS will be used in many applications with evident advantages of efficiency, performance and cost, in many cases with a significant impact on the business model of services

The applications of commercial RPAS

Photography and video:	Photogrammetry:	Inspections:	Monitoring:	Emergency management:	Logistics:
360° emotional and quality shots for the production of videos, films, marketing spots, etc.	Mapping of a large area for photographic surveys for architecture, topography, and cartography	Aerial control activities and analysis of sites, networks, remote areas or areas of high danger to humans	Aerial monitoring and supervision of large agricultural, industrial or natural areas	Urgent and exceptional transport, rescue operations in remote areas and surveillance activities in urban areas	Last mile logistics, industrial transport of spare parts or packages, urban transport of food or people

Source: Arthur D. Little (2019).

According to a recent study conducted and published by Single European Sky ATM Research/Air Traffic Management (SESAR), concerning an air traffic management system for the single European sky, approximately 7.4 million drones will be operating in the European skies by 2035. This will generate a demand of products and services worth of 10 billion euros. Growing technological innovation, new regulatory parameters, and cost containment, particularly registration and management costs are all factors that can influence market growth.

According to the same SESAR study, value-added services are expected to have the greatest economic impact in Europe in the coming years, accounting for approximately 70% of the total value along the unmanned aerial vehicle (UAV) value chain.

In terms of drone production, in all its forms and structures, Europe is one of the most important markets, with 235 active companies, 13% of which are in Italy, while the United States (US) and China dominate the market. France (Parrot), Germany (AirRobot, Ascending Technologies, and Microdrones), and Holland (Aerialtronics) are the primary civil RPAS manufacturing countries.

Finally, to complete the current publication, an in-depth investigation on the communication of innovation and innovation is proposed. In particular, methods are outlined for how communication can intervene and convey the value that is generated by technological innovation in relation to production processes to the target audiences of a company. Notably, however, the same corporate communication, business communication, is affected by new methods of transmitting information, which, in these circumstances, are also determined by digital transformation.

1. New business models in the Fourth Industrial Revolution

1. Introduction

The Fourth Industrial Revolution, also known as Industry 4.0, is concerned with the incorporation of new technologies into the industrial environment. Industry 4.0 reduces the importance of economies of scale; the strategic positioning of a company within the value chain, rather than its size or production volume, becomes increasingly important. In this sense, the digital transition alters business practices through the use of advanced technological solutions, which influence the entire production and distribution chain. This is a novel approach that considers the entire industrial cycle, with AI playing a central role in promoting integration into industrial plants.

Companies around the world are witnessing new technologies disrupt their industries, which translates into business model innovation. Companies such as Amazon, Uber, Tesla, Google, Alibaba, and UPS, among many others, have used AI to innovate their business models and improve their competitive advantages.

The concept of business model innovation has been brought to the forefront in the debate over how companies can maintain their market position; in this debate, identifying the drivers behind this maintenance process constitutes the main starting point. One factor that causes a company to innovate its business model is the influence of the external environment, particularly when this environment is of a technological nature. In this regard, there are two lines of research in the literature: one focuses on the external factors that can drive companies to engage in business model innovation; the other examines how the introduction of new technologies can involve companies innovating their business models. Unfortunately, few studies have been conducted to date on the direct impact that emerging technologies have on the evolution of business models. Only recently have some studies started meticulously exploring AI technology in the context of business model innovation (Lee, J., et al., 2019; Reim, W. et al., 2020).

Thus, to provide a holistic perspective on the methods of value creation, the present study aims to analyze the potential consequences related to the application of enabling technologies on business models. Here, a business model is understood as a set of interdependent activities that encompass the boundaries of a company.

2. Strategic innovation as a factor in new business models

The (first) financial and then economic crisis that has recently hit Italian companies (and others) and from which many are yet to emerge has accelerated a competitive evolution that was already underway. Even before the advent of the crisis, businesses were confronted with considerable strategic challenges posed by the emergence of trends that, albeit different in nature, have an impact on the evolution of enterprises. In particular, these trends can be recognized in the process of the globalization of production and outlet markets, which, by reducing the life cycle of products, increases the intensity of international competition, with a consequent margin erosion. In addition, companies must consider sociocultural aspects, such as changes in the behaviors of the average consumer who is increasingly attentive to intangible aspects such as creativity, design, and sustainability (Golinelli, 2011). Finally, the process of technological transformation, more commonly known as the advent of the Fourth Industrial Revolution, is the most influential trend; as previously highlighted, it significantly reduces the positive effects of economies of scale, allowing for the reconfiguration of products, processes, and, more generally, of value chains.

Although the digital transformation of the productive and economic system, which is now profound and irreversible, favors the creation of new development paths for companies, it also highlights the need to evolve organizational and technological structures toward new business models that are increasingly digital and interconnected.

2.1. The Fourth Industrial Revolution: Industry 4.0

The characteristics of the Fourth Industrial Revolution can be found in the ability to optimize the use of material resources through a more effective exploitation of digital technologies, which enable the creation of "smart" products and intra- and inter-company processes. This process takes place through the realization of the following.

– *Cyber-physical systems* (CPSs) are product systems (a completed product, machine, or manufacturing plant) that include both a physical and a virtual component. The physical component consists of a material device equipped with sensors, memories, connectivity, computational capacity, and actuators that allow a CPS to perceive the real world in which it moves and to interact with and control or be controlled by other material devices, both physically and virtually. The virtual component, conversely, comprises a *digital twin* of the material device (Negri, 2017). This digital copy enables, during the design phase of the material device, it to simulate its behavior to prevent errors, to support its realization by reflecting user requests and determining the optimal operating conditions, and to explore alternatives while limiting costs and risks. However, during the use phase, the digital copy enables a monitoring of its correctness and efficiency throughout its life cycle, anticipating its actual performance and identifying reusable parts upon disposal.

– *Cyber-physical production systems* (CPPSs) are production systems that comprise several CPSs as well as archiving systems in addition to those already provided to an individual CPS, which are capable of sharing data to self-monitor, self-learn, self-manage, and self-adapt. Therefore, the emphasis shifts from a single machine or manufacturing plant to the overall intra- and inter-company production flow. CPPSs are constitute the basis of the creation of an intelligent factory and its interconnection with the other actors of its *value (eco) system* as well as the *digital thread.*

The fusion of the physical world with the virtual one within the CPSs and CPPSs that characterize the Fourth Industrial Revolution is made possible by the advent of enabling technologies, such as the following:

1. **advanced manufacturing solutions** or advanced production systems; these technologies include automatic material handling systems and advanced robotics with collaborative robots;
2. **additive manufacturing** or additive manufacturing systems, such as the 3D printer;
3. **augmented reality,** which consists of vision systems that support operators in carrying out daily activities;
4. **simulation** between interconnected machines to optimize processes;
5. **horizontal and vertical integration,** which comprises the integration and exchange of information, horizontally and vertically, between all the players in a production process;
6. **industrial internet,** which involves internal communication between the elements of production within the company as well as external communication owing to the use of internet networks;
7. **cloud robotics,** which consists of the implementation of all cloud technologies such as the "online storage" of information as well as the use of "cloud computing" and external data analysis services;
8. **cyber security,** which involves overseeing the security of information and company systems that must not be altered in any way from the outside because of the new interconnections; and
9. **Big Data analytics** or techniques for managing large amounts of data through open systems that allow forecasts or predictions (Pedrazzini, 2018).

The application of these technologies inevitably affects the entire business system; these effects are unquestionably related to the use of data–and thus to the real value assumed by the same in light of the high interpretative capacity that is dictated by the aforementioned technologies–in the context of man–machine interaction and production logics.

3. The impact of new technologies on production

The typical solutions of the new production paradigm, as seen earlier, do not actually constitute an element of absolute novelty in the field of production systems; Industry 4.0 is founded not on new technologies but on their evolution and combination. There are numerous technologies that can be used in this area; while not new, these technologies can now be applied with reasonable purchase costs and sustainable integration efforts. However, the new data acquisition and analysis technologies are fundamentally altering the operation of manufacturing machines. For example, the most advanced machine tools can continuously monitor a process, suggesting better setups and generally ensuring a better performance compared to previous tools. This technological innovation in, for example, the manufacturing sector, which is strongly linked to ICT, is rapidly increasing the performance of production processes while reducing costs.

Until recently, equipping a machine with sensors that were not designed with this evolution in mind was extremely difficult owing to the costs of the technology as well as the complexity associated with adapting the technology itself. At present, however, there are extremely affordable devices that guarantee high-quality performance because these devices can be easily configured and used for a specific function.

Production systems will be able to automatically adapt to their operating conditions owing to the use of digital technologies and collected data. This can be accomplished by integrating the machine equipped with self-learning methods. In this regard, the integration of the new machines with those already in place in the company will be critical as this is a fundamental aspect to consider in order to fully understand if and how a reconfiguration process for production can be activated (Mercuri, 2020).

The integration process plays a decisive role in the interaction between man and machine. This interaction accounts for the possibility of incorporating advanced machines that are capable of integrating with one another and interacting with humans, such as robots, into production processes. The latter, called cobots, can share the same space as the operators and physically interact with humans without the need for physical safety devices like cages and photocells, which are standard in any industrial plant. Cobots are useful for situations in which the processing is so delicate that a simple machine cannot handle it and is so repetitive that the operator becomes alienated. Furthermore, the collaborative interaction between man and machine enables the development of new services to improve the working conditions of the employees involved in such interactions.

Redesigning systems and interfaces that are capable of adapting to the abilities of the person interacting with them is one of the possibilities offered by the redesign of work environments with an eye toward Industry 4.0. The goal is to reduce the likelihood of errors and, potentially, the number of major and injuries in the workplace. Among the various human–machine interfaces, "chatbot" technology plays a notable role. Chatbots are programs that can hold a conversation in natural language. Currently, chatbots are commonly used as "personal assistants" that can simplify interactions regarding external services, such as in retail, food, fashion, or healthcare. It should be noted that chatbot technology entails more than merely understanding natural language–in effect, a chatbot is an AI that is capable of learning from interactions with humans and proposing new solutions that are appropriate to the industrial context in which it operates.

There are numerous examples of how the use of cobots in manufacturing is becoming increasingly widespread; for example, Volkswagen has incorporated an industrial robotic arm from the Danish manufacturer Universal Robots into the engine production of its Salzgitter plant in Germany since 2013.

Fig. 1.1. UR5 Robot Used in Volkswagen

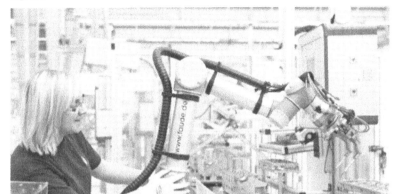

Source: www.automazione-plus.it, "A collaborative robot for Volkswagen engines,"
2013.

The UR5 robot, as shown in the figure, was installed in the department dedicated to cylinder heads, where it delicately handles candles. It was the first collaborative robot to be introduced in Volkswagen factories around the world. Representatives of the German car manufacturer specified the following: "Through this project[,] we would like to create an ergonomic work environment to avoid long-term pathologies for employees who work in every sector of the company. The robots without fences can work alongside the workers and, in this way, become real production assistants, saving staff from ergonomically heavier tasks."

Industry 4.0 also includes some technologies that, when used in production, have interesting safety implications. Radio frequency identification (RFID) and near field communication (NFC) are two such examples. RFID allows an electronic label known as a TAG to store data and, if required, communicate it to readers. NFC, by contrast, is a far more specialized subset of RFID technology: it, too, uses radio waves for communication; however, it only allows two-way communication between two devices and only works if the devices are considerably close to each other (an optimal distance of 3–4 centimeters) but without the need for contact. This technology has entered common use since the inception of contactless payment cards.

The aforementioned technologies can contribute substantially to production and worker safety, for example, by serving as an access key to perform specific functions, such as restricting access to dangerous areas within a company to authorized and appropriately trained employees who wear a badge with an RFID or NFC TAG. Because TAGs can store data, TAGs can also be used to track a product along the production and assembly phases. It is possible to remember the status of a product by updating the TAG each time a new machining operation is performed on it. Thus, we can remain aware of the operations that the semi-finished product in question has undergone and of the issues that might have arisen during the production cycle (Cervelli, 2017)

Analyzing a specific aspect of production, such as quality control, highlights that this phase is carried out on a sample basis in most SMEs (Smal and Medium-sized Enterprises) by developing an ad hoc control or by using machines that are specifically designed for the product variant to be checked. These solutions, however, are typically rigid and thus incapable of adapting to different productions, which indicates the need to innovate control methods to cope with the flexibility of new production machines, which can produce both small and large batches and therefore potentially always different products.

One alternative to obsolete technologies is the use of computer vision, which can be a valuable tool for improving quality control and making it more flexible and comprehensive. In particular, an artificial vision system can be programmed to detect certain parameters based on the lot that the machines produce, allowing the control to be transformed from a sample to the total amount.

Further, when it comes to processing control, the concept of Industry 4.0 becomes synonymous with that of a *smart factory*; by smart, we mean the withdrawal of people from repetitive and low-value-added operations, which are instead delegated to machines or robots. The operator is entrusted with a more professionalizing task, which comprises managing the artificial vision systems remotely, configuring them for the specific product being manufactured, and supervising the proper operation of the entire process. In this manner, the operational activity can be delegated to the robot, while the setting of the parameters remains in the hands of an operator, whose duties and professionalism will be enhanced.

In addition, another aspect on which the Fourth Industrial Revolution will have an impact involves the instruments used to measure company performance. These become more prevalent over time and become part of a wide range of activities to make all the events that occur within a company more understandable. In this context, a company that adopts these systems can provide greater assurances to its customers about the quality of its production outputs and consolidate the levers that underpin its competitive advantage. Furthermore, the development of such solutions may represent a strategic opportunity as the production and marketing of the developed measurement systems could result in the creation of new business branches.

Given the previous considerations, we can state that the production system developed according to the logic of the Fourth Industrial Revolution is characterized by a real interaction between man and machine, which results in an increase in production efficiency and new development opportunities.

The subsequent paragraphs examine the impact of new enabling technologies on the logistics sector, which is the sector most involved in testing these technologies.

3.1. The impact of new technologies on internal logistics

Inbound logistics is another area in which digital technologies can help companies evolve their processes to make them more efficient, understandable, and coordinated. The first relevant aspect in this area is the need to adopt a methodology that allows one to work in a more integrated and efficient manner. From the logistical point of view, we speak of *lean logistics*, a term derived from *lean manufacturing* that represents a process management philosophy inspired by

"Just in Time" (JIT). Recent corporate experiences show that time reduction is the primary goal of the JIT management technique, as demonstrated by the drastic reductions in production and crossing times. The Japanese philosophy enables the development of flexible, efficient, and reliable processes by ensuring constant rhythms that are not too high, no periods of inactivity, and the continuous production of goods as well as the creation of added value.

In particular, a methodology integrated into lean production theory is the *single-minute exchange of die* (SMED), which aims at reducing setup times to maximize the performance of a machine or plant by reducing the time required or involved in changing equipment, making adjustments, start-ups, breakdowns, inactive periods, micro-stops, speed, and reworking. In other words, the SMED enables a rapid switch from one product to another within the same plant.

The Industry 4.0 paradigm seems to be subject to the lean philosophy; in 4.0 companies, the real-time availability of precise data, combined with a high processing capacity of the same, favors an easier identification of the underlying causes of problems because the criticality is resolved precisely with the aid of complete and conveniently usable information.

Software technologies such as *supply chain event management* (SCEM) can help develop internal logistics management, which allows for the management of events throughout the production process of a plant or the entire logistics chain. A SCEM system synthesizes a substantial amount of analyzed data, which is then shown to the operator through appropriate web-based platforms. This can be achieved by using Kanban, RFID, barcodes, and QR codes, which are affixed to the walls or baskets that contain a predetermined number of semi-finished products and provide the data necessary for the management of events in real time, thereby limiting the deviations between the theoretical plan and the actual progress of the process. Of the aforementioned technologies, the Kanban, a tool that acts as a reminder and manages work order, reporting all the information relating to the activities that the production department must carry out, is the one that connects lean philosophy with the philosophy of Industry 4.0.

Another solution, as we have seen before, consists in the introduction of intelligent systems onboard the robots. This robotic intelligence can be managed in several ways:

- *through a centralized system*, where the processing and decision-making capacity is possessed by a central computer that makes decisions and communicates the actions that must be carried out to the robots–this system is effective only in the presence of a few robots;
- *through a distributed system* in which each robot can analyze its situation and decide on the actions that must be carried out–this is a suitable solution if numerous robots are working simultaneously; and
- *through an intermediate system*, where the robots can analyze their situations and make decisions autonomously but, if the situation proves too complex, a more powerful central computer can intervene–this is likely the most suitable solution.

The systems described above are fundamental in internal logistics for controlling all the elements in a company. Indeed, knowing the location of semi-finished products, production equipment, and finished products as well as the means of transporting goods benefits the company in terms of both safety and time optimization (Cervelli, 2017).

Logistics automation and intelligent logistics are two pillars of Industry 4.0. There are industries that can benefit from intelligent logistics because these industries have small series and products with numerous variations. For example, the use of small and agile unmanned aircraft known as "drones" might represent a valuable tool for factory logistics. In this regard, a particularly interesting aspect is the reconfigurability of the machines used for logistics. As the type of production changes, one can envision the introduction of mobile and rapidly reconfigurable robot teams that assist the operator along the production, assembly, and logistics lines. The ability to easily reconfigure these devices is of primary importance to achieve maximum flexibility, a strong point of our SMEs, and is a primary objective of Industry 4.0.

Another problem that arises in the context of the handling of goods within a company's spaces is the unloading of containers with raw materials or semi-finished or finished products that the company receives from its suppliers. This is an extremely important aspect because it often represents a bottleneck for companies' logistical activities as most unloading is performed manually by workers, consuming a substantial amount of time and resources and posing considerable risks to the safety of the workers.

To deal with this type of criticality, some robotic "auto-unloading" systems are being developed that can recognize goods by reading RFID TAGs or similar technologies and communicating with the company's management system, allowing the incoming goods to be automatically inserted into the system. With the introduction of these management elements, you can automatically prepare the pallets containing the goods received and prepare them for shipment with the labeling machines, enabling operators to manage the goods in the warehouse as efficiently as possible.

Therefore, we can conclude that introducing technologies that allow process automation is insufficient for the creation of a 4.0 internal logistics system. Rather, it is necessary to adopt a considerably robust approach that allows the company to work better, integrating information from various production or assembly stations and providing production data in advance to warehouses, sales, maintenance, and all other departments.

The internal activities of a company can then be improved using simulation software, which consists of systems that identify and display an abstract model that represents the real functioning of one or more processes and allows one to vary the parameters to evaluate the impact thereof. This area has advanced software that also includes functions that help ascertain the best scenario, thus providing valid decision support. For example, suppose that a company in the manufacturing sector is in a position to have numerous failures, prolonged setup times, and a completely inefficient production system. To improve the process, the company may decide to implement a simulation system that allows it to analyze the situation and obtain tangible improvements through the use of software that can simulate and analyze process behavior. This technology would let the company detect, for example, the existence of a bottleneck owing to specific machinery, which the management was previously unaware of because their information was inaccurate and outdated. Such a scenario is an example of how, hypothetically, new technologies can benefit an entire company by allowing the identification of critical issues while increasing both process know-how and the management's level of knowledge regarding their own business.

3.2. The impact of new technologies on external logistics and after-sales services

After analyzing the effects of new enabling technologies on internal logistics, it is necessary to investigate the aspects that characterize their applicability to external logistics and after-sales services. Too often, manufacturing companies fail to recognize the benefits of managing external logistics. For some companies, what happens before the goods arrive in their warehouse or after the products are delivered is unimportant because such companies are too often focused on what happens within the company itself. In reality, in a context such as the present one, where competitiveness is defined by the pursuit of maximum efficiency, the management of external logistics (and thus of the extended value chain) plays an increasingly important role (Barile et al., 2012). One of the major benefits of integrating all phases of the supply chain, for example, is the availability of information, which in Industry 4.0 is reflected in the presence of a system for collecting, processing, and analyzing data.

Big Data is one of the latest generation technologies that is becoming increasingly important in external logistics. Big Data analysis enables companies to develop real-time strategies based on precise and timely market information. Numerous opportunities emerge because of the use of these technologies, which a company can capitalize on, such as the following:

- its customers can automatically reorder goods to ensure their availability or to avoid excessive inventories of a product in the warehouse;
- market preferences can be studied for future product redesigns; and

– production and orders for raw materials can be rescheduled more efficiently based on sales trends.

The aspects described above merely represent a few examples, but the benefits that 4.0 solutions can bring to external logistics are innumerable and affect all the players in the chain, beginning with the raw material suppliers and ending with the final customer. Although the concepts expressed herein have been studied for several years now, it is the technologies of a 4.0 company that allow them to be implemented quickly and easily.

In addition, the use of modeling and process simulation techniques can improve external logistics. Through the use of these new digital technologies, precise and reliable simulations of the entire supply chain, from the supplier of raw materials to the distributor, are becoming increasingly feasible. The relationships between the aforementioned subjects within the supply chain were previously rigid owing to the inability of technologies to manage the system's complexity but can now be fully exploited because of Industry 4.0, for example, through the use of *process mining*. This is a methodology that is based on the idea of modeling, monitoring, and improving processes by extracting knowledge from logs, which are now widely available in information systems. Logs contain information about the execution of processes in the real world, which is essential for developing strategies to improve the quality of processes and reduce costs. In practice, process mining applications allow for the automatic extraction of a process model starting from a log (*discovery*); conformity checking (*conformance checking*), namely, the identification of any discrepancies between a process model and the information contained in a log; the identification and organization of social networks (*social networks*); the automatic construction of simulation models; the extension and revision of models; and the prediction of the possible future evolutions of a process instance (Van Der Aalst et al., 2012). Ultimately, we can say that process mining is a technology that supports business intelligence techniques, that is, the entire set of business processes designed to collect data and analyze strategic information.

4. The impact of Industry 4.0 on business models

The dimensions that Industry 4.0 seems to affect, at the company level, can be traced back to technical and operational aspects (man–machine integration, quality, etc.) as well as managerial aspects (work–life style, greater access to information, etc.); the implementation of the new Industry 4.0 industrial paradigm connects technological innovation with the evolution of business models, which can essentially be grouped into four broad categories: *smart factory, servitization, data-driven,* and *platform.*

Although the previous analysis focused on the manufacturing industry and logistics, Industry 4.0 must be considered a viable basis for proposing new solutions in different industrial sectors or even creating a new business (a combination of sectors/markets).

The possibility of creating new businesses, or even modifying existing ones, can be evaluated based on innovative start-ups or existing companies that are already present on the market. Unlike the latter, which sometimes tend to focus solely on the mere improvement of existing products and processes, innovative start-ups are often the firms that redefine the limits of traditional businesses. The opportunities provided by the Fourth Industrial Revolution to develop new business models are genuine incentives for innovation and the acquisition of new market shares. In other words, adopting Industry 4.0 tools is an opportunity to innovate one's "how to" strategy and diversify from competitors rather than a benefit to recover operational efficiency.

The introduction of such a concept is fundamental for smaller companies, which have a great opportunity to intercept latent needs and even create new ones through the development of innovative business models while avoiding the market balance often dictated by large companies. Furthermore, the adoption of enabling technologies and a propensity for innovation can enable these smaller companies to create new organizational and operational balances within the supply chains in which they operate, moving from a non-integrated model to a smart and interconnected ecosystem aimed at promoting a product and/or an increasingly competitive service.

In conclusion, the Fourth Industrial Revolution has the potential to radically increase the competitiveness of the national production system; however, this objective must be considered consequential to the exploitation of the opportunities associated with the new industrial paradigm.

2. The new frontiers of remote sensing

1. Introduction and the definition of remote sensing

Remote sensing enables the collection of qualitative and quantitative data regarding a specific reference context as well as methods, techniques, and tools that can be used in the subsequent stages of preparation, processing, and interpretation (Fussell, Rundquist, & Harrington, 1986; Campbell & Wynne, 2011). Remote sensing makes it possible to describe the largest feasible number of components present on a given territory, ensuring that these components are appropriately distinguished from each other. This is accomplished through the use of several sensors that collect data that are transmitted by the electromagnetic energy emitted, reflected, or diffused by analyzed objects. Specifically, this process is based on how the surfaces of objects interact with the electromagnetic energy emitted by a source that is used to obtain data on the peculiarities of the objects (Short, 2003). The interaction between the energy and the surface of the objects is continuously traced, generating the so-called spectral signature. Multiple spectral signatures are stored and measured by sensors mounted on satellites or airplanes. The data collected through these instruments are analyzed to obtain useful information units and make appropriate decisions. The final result is usually the production of maps that are useful for studying a specific context (Reese, 2013).

2. Remote sensing platforms and tools

2.1. The "means of transport": platforms

In remote sensing, one of the main characteristics used to measure the electromagnetic energy emitted or reflected by the observed object/territory is the distance from the target to be observed. This distance depends on the type of platform used in the observation (Pepe, Fregonese, & Scaioni, 2018). The term "platform" refers to the "means of transport" for the instruments or sensors used for observation (Toth & Jóźków, 2016). Thus, the platforms determine the sensor's distance from the planet's surface (e.g., planes and satellites) (Kerle, 2004). There are three classes of platforms in terms of the perspective and observation altitude: *ground platforms, aircraft platforms*, and *satellite platforms* (Matese et al., 2015). *Ground platforms* are attached to the earth's surface and have the shortest observation range (e.g., vehicles with mobile arms, metal towers, or trestles). *Aircraft platforms* are positioned at altitudes between 300 and 15,000 meters. From these shots, it is possible to obtain a stereoscopic vision (3D) of the territory that allows for accurate maps to be produced and altimetric and Plano-altimetric measurements to be performed with precision. Finally, satellite platforms are satellites that are used to observe the earth from space as well as to perform repetitive and systematic monitoring of large areas of land. A satellite is a celestial and artificial body that rotates around a planet with a trajectory, called an orbit, and depends on the force of attraction between two bodies (gravity) and centrifugal force. Artificial satellites are launched at a specific speed to achieve the equilibrium position of these two forces and in the areas of the atmosphere where friction forces are zero. Data from satellite platforms are considerably useful for the continuous monitoring of the terrestrial globe. Satellites, in particular, enable periodic shots of territories, which is essential in sectors such as meteorological forecasting. Satellites can be manned or unmanned. The type of data and the frequency of the acquisition of the satellites depend on the orbital characteristics. There are two main categories of satellites: geostationary and polar satellites. Geostationary satellites are most commonly used for telecommunications or meteorology; their main characteristic is that these satellites travel at the same angular speed as the earth. Thus, these satellites can always observe the same portion of a given territory. Polar satellites, conversely, are widely used in remote sensing studies for earth observation. They have an approximately 90 ° inclination to the equator and travel in a sun-synchronous (elliptical) orbit that takes them over the two terrestrial poles at regular intervals.

2.2. Sensors as "observation tools"

Remote sensing sensors are divided into two large groups (Borfecchia et al., 2010): *active sensors* and *passive sensors*. Active sensors record the electromagnetic energy that is emitted by the surfaces and generate the energy that is required to illuminate the scene to be filmed (e.g., radars consist of a transmitter that emits an electromagnetic wave beam and a receiver that measures the intensity of the return radiation (backscattering radiation) that is diffused by the bodies on the ground). Conversely, passive sensors do not emit energy but exclusively exploit the natural radiation of other light sources (e.g., radiometers measure the energy coming from external sources such as the sun in the visible band or the earth in the thermal infrared bands).

Naturally, the information that is collected by passive optical sensors and active radars is different; therefore, the two types of information must be considered complementary for a more detailed description of the environmental conditions of a given territory to be obtained. The sensors, whether active or passive, detect the spectral imprint of the observed surface. To a considerable extent, the sensors can distinguish different types of territories (e.g., it is possible to distinguish a water body from an agricultural field) and the state of the surfaces and objects comprising the given territory (the water quality of a water body, the state of vegetation in a field, the presence of certain minerals in rocks, etc.) by measuring the energy that is emitted or reflected at different wavelengths. One characteristic that distinguishes remote sensing as a highly versatile and widely used technique for earth observation is the ability to perform multispectral analyses (to acquire multiple images simultaneously, one for each spectral portion that the sensor can acquire, and then interpret the same object at different wavelengths). These spectral portions, defined by lower and higher wavelength values, are referred to as spectral bands. The acquisition of images in different bands enables an analysis of the various properties of the surfaces under investigation owing to specific responses in the different portions of the spectrum. The tools used for remote sensing can be classified based on the spectral bands acquired and the range of action under which they can perform the analysis. In particular, based on the type of measurement, two classes of instruments can be identified.

- *Punctual measurements*: the instruments in this category allow for punctual and considerably high-resolution analyses. These tools are applied on mobile ground platforms (e.g., vehicles, radio-controlled models or backpack-loaded on specialized personnel, etc.). These tools are extremely useful for analyzing minute portions of the surface or correcting and calibrating the data detected by satellite or aircraft. Typical instruments for point measurements are radiometers and spectrometers. Radiometers either measure radiant energy from a single spectral region or operate in multiple spectrum bands simultaneously (multispectral radiometers). Radiometers that are capable of measuring radiant energy simultaneously in many (50–200) contiguous spectral bands are called spectroradiometers. Radiometers and spectroradiometers are indispensable tools for remote sensing. Their use enables the collection of precise radiance measurements.
- *Spatial measurements:* the instruments in this category are all sensors that are typically mounted on aerial and satellite platforms. These instruments have a wider acquisition range and a resolution of up to 10 centimeters. Cameras and scanners are among the tools used for spatial measurements. Geometric and chromatic data are provided by the cameras, which have an optical element (lens) that consist of a set of lenses, which are capable of directing light toward the film; a light meter, which allows for the intensity of light entering the camera to be controlled; a shutter for the exposure time of the film; and an aperture, which adjusts

the amount of light that enters the camera. Scanners are scanning radiometers that can scan an entire "scene" line by line and generate a two-dimensional image of the area being photographed. In particular, through an optical system, scanners collect electromagnetic energy from the scene and transform it into electrical signals through detectors.

2.3. The technical characteristics of remote sensing tools

One of the peculiarities of remote sensing is the synoptic view of large portions of the territory (Xu et al., 2016). Specifically, remotely sensed data, particularly those derived from scanners, are organized into digital images. A digital image corresponds to a matrix of discrete elements called pixels (picture elements): the smaller a pixel is, the greater the details "contained" in the image are. The intrinsic properties of digital images depend on the characteristics of the sensors and platforms used to acquire the data (characteristics that are called "resolutions"). There are four types of resolution in a scanning system: geometric, radiometric, spectral, and temporal. Geometric resolution refers to the minimum area that is visible via the instrument; it is given as an instantaneous field of view (IFOV) or, given a certain distance between the sensor and the surface, as the ground area underlying a given IFOV (Poropat, 1993). By radiometric resolution, we mean the minimum energy that is capable of stimulating the sensitive element to produce an electrical signal detectable by the equipment. Further, spectral resolution indicates the range of the wavelengths to which the instrument is sensitive. Finally, temporal resolution refers to the time interval between two successive surveys of the same area. There is no single sensor that can have the best features in all resolutions. Let us imagine we have a sensor with a high geometric resolution. These sensors are characterized by a small IFOV that enables the vision of a small portion of soil and the collection of a small amount of energy. Increasing the amount of energy that the sensor receives is made possible by decreasing the spectral or radiometric resolution. Therefore, evidently, when designing a sensor, the different resolutions must be balanced according to the lens, the type of surfaces to be investigated, and the operational characteristics of detection (Giacinto, Roli, & Bruzzone, 2000).

3. From images to maps: remote sensing techniques and methods

Information concerning the nature and state of an observed territory must be extracted from remote sensing images using appropriate analyses and interpretations. For this purpose, the data collected through methods, techniques, and tools are adequately processed to obtain useful information regarding the investigated surfaces. The process generally produces maps that provide useful information for those involved in environmental research, monitoring, and management. A remote sensing image captured using digital tools corresponds to a matrix of discrete elements known as pixels, the dimensions of which are determined by the sensor and the distance from the surface.

The combination of different images of different bands can be in true color (a combination of colors similar to that perceived by the human eye) if the red, green, and blue bands are loaded into their respective channels or in false color if any other combination of bands is displayed.

It should be noted that remote sensing tools allow for the expansion of optical vision into other portions of the electromagnetic spectrum. Remote sensing, in particular, allows for the visualization of the computer triplets of bands belonging to the portions of the spectrum not visible to the human eye, allowing for a more in-depth investigation of a given territory.

3.1. The statistical analysis of remote sensing images

The gray levels detected in the images are a graphical representation of radiant energy measurements. By analyzing these measures using a histogram, an image can be treated as a statistical population of radiance or reflectance values. In particular, a graph that "measures" the number of times the same DN value appears within the same scene can be constructed. First, the histogram provides the image fashion. It consists of the DN values that have the maximum frequency. Second, the histogram provides the average value of the image, which gives an idea of its brightness: if the value is low, the image is expected to be represented with dark gray levels corresponding to low radiance values; if the value is high, the opposite occurs. Finally, the histogram provides the variance of the image, namely, the contrast of the image.

Thus, the histogram enables the extraction of some essential elements for the analysis of the remote sensing area (Chen & Ho, 2008).

3.2. Image enhancement techniques and vegetation indices

The quality of images recorded on digital media is often inadequate. The techniques that allow for these limits to be overcome are as follows:

- contrast stretching, where the contrast of an image is increased, which requires an operation that directly affects the signal's range, and
- brightness adjustment, which involves modifying the original brightness values. This operation involves a constant shift of all the gray density levels present in the scene.

Banding operations, as with image enhancement techniques, aim to create a new image from which more information can be extracted than the original. The simplest operations between bands are arithmetic ones (sum, difference, product, and ratio). The objective of these operations is to highlight the different spectral responses of the surface covers across the spectrum. The vegetation indices are also calculated in this manner. It is particularly easy to distinguish vegetated surfaces from others by dividing the IR band by the red band.

3.3. Thematic maps

The fundamental purpose of remote sensing techniques is to create a thematic map. Thematic maps provide information on specific aspects of the territory represented through appropriate symbols and colors. In particular, based on a topographical or geographical map, the aspects of the territory represented are expressed through qualitative and quantitative symbols: physical, anthropic, economic, archaeological, and land use aspects. Each represented aspect takes the name of the theme and is highlighted through appropriate graphic signs or colors.

Classification refers to the process of switching from the remote sensed starting image to the thematic map. This process can be either manual or automatic. The application domain expert performs manual classification through a visual (photo-) interpretation of the acquired images. This visual interpretation consists of the observation and comparison of images printed in a photographic or digital format. In the process of manual interpretation, some characteristic parameters of the image are analyzed.

- The tone corresponds to the intensity level of a monochrome image or the combination of intensity levels for a multispectral (color) image.
- The shape is simply given by a geometric outline of an object.
- The size refers to the area of an object and can indicate its simple linear dimension (e.g., the length of an airport runway).
- The pattern represents the shapes of objects in space.
- The texture describes the structure of the spatial variations of brightness within an element and determines the smooth or rough appearance of a certain surface.
- The location indicates both the geographical position of an object and the position of an element relative to others.

Manual classification differs from automatic classification. The latter is carried out by a computer, which assigns to each pixel of the image the class or category to which it belongs based on its spectral characteristics: groups of pixels with similar spectral behavior are classified as belonging to the same class. Unsupervised classification and supervised classification are the two types of automatic classifications. Unsupervised classifications organize pixels into clusters or groups without relying on a direct knowledge of the process. Supervised classifications are based on the ground knowledge of some areas that are called sample areas, which are well located on the image and represent the coverage classes of the future thematic map. A supervised classification is articulated in three phases. The first phase consists of the training phase in which several emblematic pixels of the different interest classes are selected, and training pixels are used to train the software. Second, in the assignment phase, the decision rules that were developed during the first phase are used to associate a label to all the image pixels. In particular, all the other pixels in the image are presented to the computer one at a time through a calculation program, which assigns them a label relating to one of the thematic classes of interest. Finally, in the evaluation phase, the accuracy of the thematic map produced is checked. This verification takes place by comparing the class to which it belongs and the label that the automatic classification process has assigned to it. The mistakes made are thus evaluated in the third phase.

4. Remote sensing and 4.0 technologies: precision farming and livestock farming

In the current phase of development, agriculture and livestock farming face multiple challenges:

- the gradual decrease of the energy and primary resources currently used (oil and water above all);
- the constant increase in prices for the purchase of production factors;
- the decrease in the selling prices of agricultural and zootechnical products;
- environmental pollution;
- animal welfare; and
- the continuous and unstoppable change in the climate.

These challenges are being faced by the agricultural and zootechnical sectors, which are transitioning from a primarily productive model focused solely on meeting food needs to a model focused on improving products and protecting natural resources. Technological innovation is the means by which this change can be implemented; it enables the development of alternative solutions that can reduce long-term production costs while limiting the introduction of pollutants. The European Union also encourages this change by promoting more and more initiatives and rewards for entrepreneurs who are committed to this new direction. In this context, two new management and business systems have been perfected: precision farming and livestock farming.

Precision farming is based on methods, techniques, and tools for managing the spatial and temporal variability of agricultural production (Pierce & Nowak, 1999). It undoubtedly represents a form of advanced agriculture that captures the uniqueness of the land owing to the various covers to be used. Precision agriculture enables the input–transformation–output process to be optimized by rationalizing the available resources (Godwin & Miller, 2003).

By contrast, livestock farming refers to the use of technologies to measure the physiological, behavioral, productive, and reproductive indicators of individual animals to improve management strategies and the performance of the animals raised. It is an interdisciplinary subject that combines computer science, biostatistics, engineering, and economics to investigate zootechnical issues (production, reproduction, behavior, health, and nutrition). Zootechnics has several objectives:

- to diagnose diseases early and improve animal health, welfare, and product quality;
- to reduce the use of drugs and the environmental impact; and
- to increase production and decrease costs.

The advantages thereof are more evident in large farms, where the visual observation of a single animal is nearly impossible and the manpower used may be less qualified.

4.1. Precision viticulture

Modern viticulture is a type of precision agriculture (Matese & Di Gennaro, 2015). Precision viticulture aims to understand the interactions between the vineyard and the environment to achieve differentiated management between the different vineyards and within the vineyard itself. Precision viticulture has several operational goals. First, it aims to manage the heterogeneity of the vineyards through the differentiated fertilization of various vineyard portions using variable rate technology (VRT). Second, it aims to reduce costs and the environmental impact of treatments by using variable-rate sprayers. Third, it aims to differentiate between green pruning and leaf stripping based on vigor and microclimatic needs. Furthermore, precision viticulture can also achieve uniform batches of grapes for harvesting (selective harvest).

Remote sensing systems are the primary means for achieving these objectives effectively. The mapping of the vineyards, in particular, based on remote sensing techniques and the development of operating machines based on VRT, enable the differentiated management of vineyard portions.

4.2. The management of variability in agriculture

The production of the fields is highly uneven, and this variation is caused by various factors, including incorrect fertilizer use or poorly performed sowing. This variability is frequently caused by objective factors, such as a different amalgam of the soil or the presence of less porous areas (Huang et al., 2018).

Precision agriculture aims to understand what causes variability and, therefore, to identify the resources and the most appropriate tools for adapting the production process to a specific reality while avoiding waste. The variability is spatial (i.e., it is different here compared to there) and temporal (i.e., today is different from yesterday). The governance of variability requires that a production process, in light of the information collected, must be implemented in a diversified manner (Weiss, Jacob, & Duveiller, 2020). The collection of data is an essential step in governing variability with maximum precision. This collection allows one to identify the elements to consider when calibrating the best choices and strategies to be adopted. Data collection can be carried out using the following techniques:

- spatial references;
- geographic information systems (GISs);

- remote sensing;
- sensors and production mappings; and
- sampling.

4.3. The global positioning system (GPS)

Information regarding land must be georeferenced to provide useful and complete information about a plot. The GPS is the best tool for identifying and recording the position of an object on the earth's surface (Gao & Liu, 2001). The GPS offers the possibility of expressing the position of any point in the plot as a pair of geographical coordinates and associating information and data that relates to it. In addition, the GPS records the variability present within a given territory. The use of a GPS satellite receiver in agriculture has different applications:

- soil sampling and scouting, or the use of a satellite receiver to record the sampling points of the land and to identify and recognize them later on a map;
- the detection of borders and areas, or an operation that comprises following the edges of a plot with a satellite receiver combined with a recording instrument (e.g., a palmtop or data-logger), noting the coordinates of the vertices of the field for the calculation of the perimeter and area;
- navigation systems, or electronic driving systems that use satellite receivers that indicate the optimal route to follow using light or acoustic signals (guide bar) or that autonomously guide the machine during the straight path (semi-automatic driving); and
- the leveling of the ground, which, when combined with a satellite receiver, can accelerate and improve the precision of the procedures connected to.

4.4. The GIS

A GIS enables the acquisition, processing, and use of data pertaining to a specific territorial context. A GIS is a computer-based platform that combines digital representation with alphanumeric data derived from the analysis to be performed. A GIS consists of hardware, software, and human resources and can perform in-depth territorial diagnoses at scientific, logical, and conceptual levels. GIS technologies, in particular, enable the viewer of data on a map to associate several elements (spatial, physical, temporal, etc.) in only a graphic representation. This representation aids the comprehension of the given territory (Basso et al., 2003).

4.5. Remote sensing at the service of archaeology

The origin of remote sensing in the archaeological field can be traced back to the excavations at Persepolis in 1879. Since then, the continuous development of 4.0 technologies and remote sensing technologies has allowed archaeology to make great strides in evaluating archaeological sites. Remote sensing and photo-interpretation, in particular, have become increasingly important in carrying out preliminary investigations concerning an archaeological site. Currently, archaeological remote sensing is based on the interpretation of aerial photographs taken by satellites, aircraft, or terrestrial platforms. Archaeologists collect substantial scientific information about the environment through the photo-interpretation of these images. In particular, during the *preliminary verification phase of the archaeological site*, archaeologists can gather a large amount of geophysical, chemical, and metric information about the archaeological remains (Giardino, 2011). The archaeologist can use several remote sensing tools to investigate the territory. Each tool has a different resolution and classification methodology that works at both the microscale and macroscale. Landsat MSS and TM (up to 30 m resolution, e.g., Table I, a; b; c), SPOT (20-m multispectral resolution and 10-m panchromatic resolution, e.g., Table I, a); and SAR radiometric satellites are used at the macroscale. By contrast, aerial photography and aerial photogrammetry (RGB and panchromatic aerial photos), geophysics, centimeter GPS surveying, interferometry, and detection by total laser stations are used in microscale remote sensing (Forte, 1995, Rick, 1996). In this context, the archaeologist must have an in-depth knowledge of most existing technologies to conduct an appropriate survey.

4.6. SAR radiometric sensors

SARs are one of the most commonly used sensors in archaeology (Zink & Bamler, 1995). SAR polarimetric sensors transmit electromagnetic waves either horizontally (H, horizontal) or vertically (V, vertical) and receive return energy with polarization in H or V. Consequently, four transmission and reception combinations are made possible: HH (horizontal transmission and reception); VV (vertical transmission and reception); HV (horizontal transmission and vertical reception); and VH (vertical transmission and horizontal reception). Radar systems can transmit and receive one, two, or four of these polarizations. Depending on the case, the following combinations are possible: single polarization with HH or VV (or with HV or VH); dual polarization with HH and HV, VV and HV, or HH and VV; alternating polarization with HH and HV, alternating with VV and VH; or polarimetric with HH, VV, VH, and HV. The availability of polarimetric data is crucial for obtaining information from SAR data because each channel is more or less sensitive to certain conditions of the observed targets, enabling the recognition of some important physical and structural characteristics of illuminated surfaces. Therefore, having all four polarizations allows for diverse but complementary information to be obtained (Dore & Patruno, 2012).

3. A brief history and classification of drones

1. A brief history of the drones

The history of drones is linked with the history of UAVs. In general, the term "drone" refers to an aircraft that does not have a pilot on board. Drones were originally and primarily used for military purposes. However, the use of drones has evolved from the simple collection of information to military applications and, finally, to the uses that we know today.

The appearance of drones has changed, along with its applications, from simple balls of fabric and wood equipped with offensive weapons to the current vehicles that have their own engines, which allow them to fly and perform collateral services while doing so.

Drones date back to the eighteenth century; the first state to use them was France with the "Compagnie d'Aèrostiers," founded in 1794, for battlefield reconnaissance. Their first appearance was in June 1794 in the battle of "Fleurus" near "Charleroi." These drones were no longer used in use in 1799.

Other traces of aerostatic balloons for military use can be found in the First Italian War of Independence (1848–1849). Franz Von Uchatius, a young Austrian artillery lieutenant, used them to bomb Venice, which was unassailable by sea owing to the shallow waters of the lagoon; however, his attack failed because of the wind, which blew against the Austrians rather than toward the city.

In addition, aerostatic balloons were also used in the American Civil War (1861–1865) between Confederates and Unionists. Abraham Lincoln, the then president of the US, established the United

States Army Aerostatic Corps on June 11, 1861, to enrich the armed forces with reconnaissance, mapping, and other logistical functions. Subsequently, he summoned the well-known airman Thaddeus S. C. Lowe, who demonstrated the operation of the balloon that he designed, called "Enterprise," by flying it up to a height of 500 feet while using a telegraph, an operator, and a cable with a direct line to the White House across the street.

Lowe's creations were used in some reconnaissance war operations but ceased to operate in 1863, when Lowe resigned as Air Force Chief because of disagreements with some army commanders.

The next step in the use of flying objects as reconnaissance and aerial surveillance tools was made because of William A. Eddy's studies on kites[1]. Born in 1850, Eddy began studying and building his first kites as a teenager in New York, fascinated by how the surrounding environmental conditions could affect their flight. After finishing his university studies, he went to work for the *New York Herald*, a well-known newspaper at the time, and married Cinthya Huggins on April 21, 1887, at the age of 37. The constant business trips allowed him to continue cultivating his passion for kites through scientific journals and the acquaintances of others who were equally enthralled by these objects. In particular, the first to study kites as scientific instruments for measuring the change of winds was the Englishman Douglas Archibald, and his discoveries were published in the journal *Nature* in 1886. This study caught Eddy's attention; subsequently, in 1893, he created the "Diamond Eddy Kite," a hexagonal kite with a tail capable of flying at a height of 1500 feet, carrying heavy objects to measure the temperature at different atmospheric levels.

Another important milestone took place on May 30, 1895, when Eddy used his kites to take the first "clear" photograph from above. His work was crucial to American military supremacy in the Pacific and South America, allowing for the early acquisition of enemy military ship movements in the same area by means of the photos taken from above.

However, the first successful military use of unmanned aerostatic objects occurred in 1898, when the US attacked Manila Bay, then a Spanish colony, with a rampant use of kites for surveillance and reconnaissance purposes as well as for filming and recording, which allowed the US Navy to easily defeat the Spanish fleet.

Nevertheless, for the first traces of an airplane, one has to return to the early 20th century.

Wilbur and Orville Wright, born in Millville, Indiana, in 1867 and 1871, respectively, received a small helicopter as a gift from their father at one point that was made of paper, wood, and bamboo and was equipped with an elastic to turn the propeller. This model sparked the two brothers' passion for what would one day make them famous: airplanes.

The Wrights closely followed the studies of the German aeronautical pioneer Otto Lilienthal; when he died in a glider accident, the brothers realized that they had to focus on the design of their projects. The Wright brothers understood that it was possible to fly an object heavier than air but only with a good combination of three fundamental components: roll, pitch, and yaw. Following several unsuccessful attempts, the Wright brothers realized their dream on December 17, 1903, in Kitty Hawk, achieving the first prolonged, controlled, and motorized flight in the history of a heavier-than-air winged aircraft, which the brothers called the "Wright Flyer" (also known as Flyer I, Flyer 1903, or Kitty Hawk).

"Flyer I" was followed by "Flyer II," which was unsuccessful. However, on October 5, 1905, "Flyer III" flew over the fields of the Huffman Prairie for 39 minutes, covering the same distance and making some turns.

All these tests were conducted behind closed doors because the Wright brothers believed that their projects would one day make them famous and did not want them to be "copied" by experts with similar goals. With the outbreak of the First World War in 1914, the most sophisticated technologies were used, supplied to armies, for tanks, telephones, armored vehicles, and automatic firearms; the airplane became the primary air weapon in this context.

During the early years of the war, Orville Wright (his brother Wilbur died in 1912) and Charles F. Kettering made an unmanned airplane that was supposed to be used on battlefields in Europe; however, it was not perfected in time for use during the war. The prototype had a four-cylinder engine that could travel 80 kilometers per hour. A small gyroscope mounted onboard piloted the aircraft. To calculate the distance traveled, an onboard odometer was installed, which, once the target was reached, sent the command to a lever, which turned off the engine and released the wings of the fuselage, causing the explosive-equipped aircraft to crash into enemy troops.

Although the tests yielded more positive than negative results, the army saw little potential in the prototype, which is why it was never used on the battlefield. In 1916, the UK attempted to build a remotely controlled UAV, called "Aerial Target," to compete with the German airship "Zeppelin." The aircraft was built by the "Royal Aircraft Factory," but the various tests conducted were unsuccessful. The project was thus shelved but then resumed in the following years.

The "Zeppelin," which was invented by the German Ferdinand Von Zeppelin, was a rigid hydrogen airship. In 1910, airships had appeared for commercial purposes because of the first airline in the world: the "DeutscheLuftschiffahrts – AG." Following the outbreak of the First World War, the airship was transformed into a real war aircraft that was destined to create casualties and cause damage to enemy cities. The "Zeppelin," which had proved too vulnerable to gunshots from the ground, was immediately replaced by the "Z VI" and succeeded by the various "Z VII, ZVIII, and ZIX." The airships were the protagonists of several bombings such as those on the Belgian cities of Liège and Antwerp, on August 5 and 25, 1914, respectively.

The first air raids occurred between 1915 and 1918, with over 50 attacks in the UK alone, resulting in casualties, injuries, and damages estimated at hundreds of thousands of pounds. In March 1918, the city of Naples and the port of Bagnoli were also hit by German dirigibles.

Having caused fear and destruction, the airships were the subject of discussion during the armistice; their use was banned, and the confiscation of the remaining aircraft that were still operational was ordered.

Before the Treaty of Versailles was signed in June 1919, some German troops destroyed their "Zeppelins" to prevent the victorious allies from confiscating and "copying" them for the benefit of their armies. To find the first significant trace of an unmanned aircraft after World War I, it is necessary to consider September 1925, when the "British Royal Navy" designed the "RAE Larynx."

This prototype was equipped with a radial engine and a control gyroscope, allowing it to reach speeds of up to 320 kilometers per hour, a record for a war aircraft. The "RAE Larynx" was based on the same principles as the "Aerial Target," which Archibald Low designed in the UK in 1916 to combat German airships.

In the 1930s, technology made considerable strides, and the number of UAVs increased exponentially.

The term "drone" was first used by US Admiral William H. Standley in 1935 after he witnessed the British Navy's new radio-controlled aircraft in flight during an exercise. The prototype was the DH.82B Queen Bee. Back in the US, he reported what he had seen to Commander Fahrney. The term "drone" means "hum" or "male bee" in English owing to the similarity of the aircraft engines' noise to the hum of the bee.

The "Queen Bee" was made mainly of fir wood and plywood and was equipped with wheels or floats according to the launch station. It was capable of flying up to 4,000 meters high and reaching a top speed of 160 kilometers per hour. Used by the "Royal Air Force" and the "Royal Navy," these drones were decommissioned in 1947, after around 300 copies had been produced.

The first large-scale drones were built in the US. Reginald Denny, a Hollywood actor, realized his passion for radio-controlled model airplanes in 1934 by founding Reginald Denny Industries, which opened a shop that sold only these models. The shop was later renamed the Radioplane Company.

Denny was also aware of the military potential of these airplanes. In 1938, he purchased the design of Walter Righter, an American mechanical engineer who owned a small engine company, and began marketing the first radio-controlled models.

The first major drone model was known as the "Radioplane OQ-2" and was introduced in 1940. In total, 15,000 copies were produced. The model was built by the Radioplane factory in Van Nuys, California, and was used as a target in US military exercises.

One curious fact is linked to the aforementioned factory and, thus, to the history of drones: in June 1945, while visiting the factory, a US army photographer, David Conover, noticed a worker at an assembly line and photographed her by inviting her to attempt a career as an actress. Her name was Norma Jane Mortenson, but she later became famous in Hollywood under the name of Marylin Monroe.

During the Second World War, the first traces of Italian unmanned aircraft were discovered in the summer of 1942. The Italian Air Force was one of the most advanced in the old continent, relying on 18 manufacturers, including FIAT. The "Savoia-Marchetti SM.79 Sparviero" (S.M.79) bomber was the Italian army's leading aircraft.

The "S.M.79" was used successfully in the Ethiopian campaign in 1935, contributing to the nationalists' victory in the Spanish Civil War, in which Italy allied with Germany.

It was a prelude to the Second World War.

The Italian bomber "S.M.79" could reach a maximum speed of 435 kilometers per hour, fly approximately 2,000 kilometers, and carry an explosive load of 1,250 kilos. In the summer of 1942, Anglo-American allies took part in Operation Pedestal by sending a convoy bound for Malta to help the island under attack. On August 10, 13 merchant ships and two tankers were escorted by the Royal Navy and set sail from Gibraltar. Among the planes sent to intercept them were 74 S.M.79s, which inflicted heavy losses on the convoy while failing to prevent enemy ships from landing in Malta. Because of the Italian bombers, the Allies lost nine merchant ships, an aircraft carrier, and a destroyer. It was during this "Sparrowhawk" operation that Italy attempted its first unmanned aircraft attack. Ferdinando Raffaelli, the general of "Squadra Aerea," proposed equipping the "S.M.79" with explosives and a remote radio control command. The operation's target comprised the British ships that were escorting the "Operation Pedestal" to the Algerian coast.

The "Sparrowhawk" was immediately followed by another lead bomber and five "FIAT G.50" fighters that took off from the Villacidro airport in Sardinia. Marshal Francesco Badii was aboard the "S.M.79" and, after determining the aircraft's route, jumped with a parachute, leaving the pilot aircraft accompanying him with the remote radio control command. The flight was aborted owing to failure in the aircraft's transmitter, which stopped responding to commands, crashed at an altitude of 1,800 meters in Algerian territory on Mount Kenchela. The first Italian experiment with an unmanned aircraft attack was, therefore, a failure.

The "Sparrowhawk" was used, even after the end of the war, by the Italian Social Republic, an ally of the Germans, and by the co-belligerent Air Force, which was part of the allied forces.

In 1960, the Ryan Aeronautics Company in California was a leader in aerial targets, and the most famous unmanned drones at the time were those of the Teledyne Ryan Firefly/Firebee family, which have remained among the most produced target gifts to date. Owing to their success with target drones, the company was also asked to develop a surveillance variant, which flew for the first time in 1964.

Some versions of the Firefly served in Vietnam on surveillance and reconnaissance missions, such as battle damage assessment.

With more than 7,000 built across all variants, Firefly/Firebee drones are the precursors of all modern drones.

Many are still used in armies around the world, and some were also used in 2003 during the invasion of Iraq, where the drones flew in front of manned planes to establish corridors for passage.

The technological developments that have taken place over the years have made drones a more reliable solution for reconnaissance operations, leading, among other things, to the widespread diffusion of the Predator drone; owing to its ability to fly for long periods at high altitudes, this drone was born as a simple reconnaissance device. However, the first armed versions appeared in around 2001 and remain in use to date.

2. The classification of the drones

Drones are usually classified by either configuration or size. The configuration can be divided into two main types:

- fixed-wing, as with traditional airplanes, in which an upward thrust is created by moving the wings forward in the air, or
- rotors, as in helicopters, where the wings (rotors) rotate to provide thrust.

In relation to their classification by size/mass, small or considerably small drones are usually those below 7 kilograms of total mass (the maximum weight limit below which there are not too many regulations).

2.1. Fixed-wing drones

Fixed-wing aircraft use a propulsion source (typically an electric motor and a propeller) to generate thrust on their wings, thereby allowing them to fly. There are several configurations for fixed-wing aircraft, which depend on a combination of numerous factors, including the wind position, number of wings, fuselage style, control surface, and tail (or tail) style. When an aircraft is in flight, its attitude can change along three axes: the pitch axis, which causes the aircraft to tilt up and down; the yaw axis, which causes the direction to change; and the roll axis, which causes the aircraft to tilt left and right.

To control a fixed-wing aircraft, the wing and tail sections have some flaps that are called control surfaces.

There are three main control surfaces: the ailerons that control the roll of the aircraft, a rudder that controls the yaw, and the balancers that control the pitch.

Regardless of the wing arrangement of a fixed-wing aircraft, another classification is based on the position of the engine.

In most cases, the motors are located at the back of the aircraft: in this case, we refer to thrust configurations because the engine propels the aircraft forward.

Thrust motor configurations are relatively popular for use with drones because these configurations keep the propeller out of the cameras' field of view when the cameras are oriented forward.

In traction configurations, the motor and propeller are mounted at the front. This is a more traditional configuration and can be slightly more efficient than a thrust configuration because the air that hits the propeller is not disturbed by the aircraft's fuselage.

Because this configuration is usually mounted in front of the cameras, the photographs have an annoying rolling shutter effect with a strange linear design. However, this is not a problem for downward-pointing cameras (such as those used in APRs – Automatic Position Reporting System) to create maps).

The *conventional configuration* includes a single engine positioned at the front (pulling) and rear (pushing) of the aircraft. Large central wings are followed by a tail section.

Flying wings (or full wings) comprise another popular configuration owing to the fewer components and greater ease of transport involved therein.

Flying-wing drones are also more efficient and cut the wind more easily than other types of drones.

A flying wing only has two control surfaces, so it only requires two servo motors, whereas more traditional aircraft typically require four.

The control surfaces on the flying wing are called elevons because these control surfaces combine the functions of an elevator (for pitching up and down) and an aileron (for rolling the aircraft left and right).

An onboard automatic control determines how far each control surface must be moved to perform the desired action.

Flying wings are ideal for drones because there is plenty of space for all the equipment; in addition, the motors and propellers are mounted at the back, out of sight of the camera.

The main disadvantage, however, is that the center of gravity is more sensitive than in the other configurations, making flying wings more difficult to fly without an autopilot.

In addition, the placement of equipment can also be limited at times because flying-wing aircraft do not have much space to place the devices further forward or further back to keep the center of gravity in its optimal position.

Double-beam aircraft have the tail section connected to the main body (known as the fuselage) with two beams.

Similar to flying-wing propellers, thrust motors are ideal for use on double-beam drones because the propeller does not obstruct the view of forward-facing photos/cameras.

In addition, the double-beam configuration, which retains a traditional tail section, is more stable and easier to fly than a flying wing.

There are several variants of double-beam aircraft; the most common has an inverted V-tail shape, which has the advantage of having only two control surfaces (rather than three as per a regular double beam), thereby requiring only two servos. Furthermore, the inverted V-tail configuration is also more aerodynamically efficient.

2.2. Rotary-wing aircraft (rotorcraft)

The term "rotorcraft" refers to aircraft that can fly by spinning a rotor that generates sufficient lift. Rotorcraft are classified into two types: multirotors and traditional helicopters. The number of engines that are used by a multirotor determines its classification; for example, a quadcopter has four engines, while a hexacopter has six engines. Each type is discussed in depth as follows.

A *conventional helicopter* can fly by changing the pitch and angle of its rotor blades. This is accomplished through a complex mechanism called a "swashplate."

Most helicopters have a single and considerably large rotor, which creates torque in the direction that is opposite to its rotation.

This is why a tail rotor that opposes the yaw to keep the helicopter in the right direction is required.

Consequently, this design is seen as somewhat inefficient because some of the energy is used merely to keep the helicopter pointed in the same direction rather than to contribute to lifting.

To compensate for this effect, some helicopters have been designed with two blades rotating in opposite directions to neutralize the effect of torque and use all the energy to generate lift.

Typically, the naming conventions for multicopters follow the Latin numbering system: the prefix *tri-* denotes three engines, *quad-* denotes four, *hex-* denotes six, and so on, followed by the suffix -*copter*.

Tricopters, therefore, use three motors that are arranged in a triangular pattern: one at the back and two at the front. The arms of a tricopter are typically separated by 120 °, which is an advantage when using an onboard camera because this wide separation means that the propellers are outside the camera's field of view.

Another advantage is that tricopters are less expensive to build because these multicopters require three motors; however, to fully control them, the rear motor must tilt to the side to rotate the rotors left and right (yaw).

This also means that tricopters can yaw much faster than other configurations such as quadcopters.

Quadcopters, which comprise the most common type of multi-rotor drone, have four motors that are arranged symmetrically in a + or X configuration.

In a + configuration, the front of the quadcopter is directly aligned with a motor; conversely, in an X configuration, it is directly between the two front engines.

The latter configuration is more useful and common because the arms and propellers are less visible when a forward-facing camera is mounted onboard.

Two of a quadcopter's four motors rotate clockwise, while the other two rotate counterclockwise. This setting balances the torque that is generated by the motors and keeps the quadcopter pointed in the right direction (thus fulfilling the same function as the tail rotor on a traditional helicopter).

The motor speeds are varied to control the quadcopter; for example, to tilt a quadcopter forward, the two front motors slow down while the two rear ones accelerate.

Six engines power the hexacopter. Aside from the obvious fact that having more engines allows you to lift more equipment, an additional benefit is that the engines are closer together and, unlike a tricopter or quadcopter, the hexacopter usually succeeds in remaining relatively stable, using the other engines and allowing landing.

Because of the additional weight to carry and the redundancy provided by multiple motors, professional aerial photography drones typically employ six- or eight-rotor configurations.

Finally, the Y6 configuration is a mix between a tricopter and a hexacopter.

It has six motors on three arms that are mounted like a tricopter, with two arms at the front at an angle of 120° and a single arm at the rear. However, the Y6 multicopters are considered hexacopters because they have six engines in total.

Two motors are mounted on each arm: one above and one below. This configuration is called "coaxial." Typically, each motor turns in a direction that is opposite to the other.

Y6 configurations have some advantages compared to traditional hex-rotors.

Because this configuration only involves three arms and six motors, the motors have more redundancy because of how the motors are mounted, with each pair acting on the same thrust axis.

If an engine were to stop running in the Y6 configuration, the only difference would be a one-sixth reduction in thrust.

The Y6 frames have a slight disadvantage in that the lower engines work in the turbulent air that is pushed down by the upper engines, resulting in a marginal loss of efficiency (approximately 5%).

However, this reduction in efficiency is offset by the lightness of the chassis (only three arms instead of six).

Octocopters have eight evenly spaced engines and are among the largest multirotors: the typical aircraft has a diameter of 1 meter.

As with the hexacopters, the increase in the number of motors implies the possibility of carrying greater loads and having more redundant motors.

While a hexacopter can usually withstand the failure of one motor (or even two if the motors are in opposite positions), an octocopter can withstand the failure of multiple motors without falling depending on the load and on which motors have stopped running.

Octocopters are normally used as professional drones for video shooting owing to their load capacity and engine redundancy margin.

The X8 configuration is essentially a quadcopter chassis with eight engines–a mixture of a quadcopter and an octorotor. The X8 frames have four arms, each with two motors, one mounted upward and the other downward. All X8 aircraft have the same advantages as octorotors, the first of which is the ability to lift heavy loads. The X8, as with the Y6, has the advantage of having two motors along the same thrust axis, making it even more stable in the event that one motor fails during flight.

While "x-rotor" is not an official classification, it is included here because there are numerous examples of single-engine ducted fan aircraft.

These use a single propeller to generate thrust and are controlled by small flaps under the prop that manipulate airflow to allow the drone to rotate, lean forward, etc.

These designs can be considered extremely similar to conventional helicopters because they use a single main engine to lift.

The main advantage of ducted fan aircraft is that these designs are mechanically simpler because the main rotor blades are fixed; furthermore, small flaps are used under the blades to control the drone. In addition, because the blade is enclosed in a duct, the propellers are slightly more efficient than those of the same size as the rotors of a helicopter (since the tube reduces the loss of thrust at the ends of the blades for aerodynamic reasons).

Moreover, another important aspect of ducted fans concerns safety: the ducted fans prevent screwing, the possibility of the blades dangerously hitting someone, and debris accumulation.

However, these ducts also have negative effects, starting with stability in the wind.

Owing to the size of their frontal area, ducted fan aircraft are easily moved by gusts of wind, making them unsuitable for use in high-wind conditions.

Furthermore, because the motor and blades are located at the center of the drone, the space that is available for equipment is limited.

A standard configuration begins with the drone itself, which could be a multirotor or a fixed-wing aircraft. The base platform includes an autopilot, a camera, a battery, a telematics link, and a video transmitter. On the ground is the remote control, which will be used to manually control the drone; in addition, it is possible to have a video monitor, which lets a video from the drone camera be viewed in real time. The drones also use a portable ground control (or a tablet) to monitor parameters, such as altitude and speed, and can include other features, such as a map showing where the drone is flying. This station can also be used on the ground to set waypoints and send commands to the drone, such as taking a photo.

3. Notes on the structure and functioning of drones

3.1. The structure of drones

When it comes to choosing materials for a fixed-wing drone, the most common ones are solid foam, balsa wood, and composite materials such as fiberglass and carbon fiber. However, almost all fixed-wing aircraft, for hobby purposes, are made of foam-based materials because these materials are inexpensive, lightweight, and easy to repair with a little glue. Other materials could include foams with a plastic cover to improve the strength of the aircraft, but adhesive tape can also be added to the wings and underside to protect the foam during landing. Even though this adds weight, it extends the aircraft's life, particularly when landing on rough surfaces like pebbles. Some high-end aircraft are made of carbon fiber or glass fiber, which ensures increased strength and durability. However, drones comprising these materials are more useful for experienced drone operators because they are more difficult to work with and difficult to repair the quickly in the event of an accident.

The payload area is an important component of the frame of a fixed-wing drone because it is where all the equipment is assembled. First, ensure that the area is large enough to accommodate the auto-pilot, battery, and video camera.

It is even more essential to ensure that the aircraft has sufficient space for the equipment to move forward and backward and to ensure that the center of gravity is correct. The center of gravity for most aircraft will be approximately a third of the chord from the leading edge. It is usually marked on the aircraft or listed in the assembly instructions. The exact center of gravity of a wing is difficult to calculate without going into technical aerodynamic details; however, for most aircraft, the "one-third" rule is sufficient to estimate it.

The servos on fixed-wing aircraft are primarily used as actuators to move control surfaces but can be used for other things, such as cracking a camera up or down.

Each control surface on a fixed-wing aircraft is typically controlled by a single servo, so there will be one servo for the rudder, one for the elevator, and so on. The gears inside the servos are either plastic or metal. Plastic gear servos are inexpensive and lightweight, but metal gear servos are preferable for more demanding tasks because metal gear servos can produce more torque than plastic ones. Ensure that the servo is powerful enough for the task at hand; otherwise, its gears might break, or its motor might burn out.

Depending on the size of the aircraft, it is possible to have one with detachable wings. This makes transporting or storing a drone much easier.

Most multicopters, particularly quadcopters, have a remarkable mechanical simplicity; multicopters are extremely easy to build with basic materials such as wood. Making a quadcopter from scratch using plastic parts and carbon fiber is now far more straightforward than it was a mere few years ago owing to the availability of easy-to-use 3D printers.

The center plate is the main section of a multirotor on which the arms are mounted, and it is often constructed from fiberglass or carbon fiber. To accommodate equipment, some multirotor chassis designs have multiple center plates stacked on top of one other.

The arms of a multirotor are those to which the motors are attached. Most are square or circular tubular structures; however, in some smaller multirotor frames (particularly common in mini quadcopters), the arms may be flat plates or other plastic structures. The arms of some multirotors can be removed and folded for easy transport and storage. It is often useful to have considerably stiff arms on the multirotor, but doing so significantly increases the weight of the frame, which generally has a negative impact on flight duration. When choosing a frame, the manufacturer will typically indicate the maximum weight that can be supported at takeoff, which gives an idea of the strength of the arms and what can be carried on the drone.

Many chassis include a *power distribution board* (PDB) that is built into the center plate, which makes powering equipment and motors easier. Some PDBs have additional functions, such as a voltage regulator to power other devices (e.g., video cameras) on the drone. Others include connectors for the receiver and autopilot, which help maintain the tidiness of the wiring.

PDB is a grand name for a considerably light and solid frame that has no internal structure because the structure comprises the outer layer itself. This type of frame can be found in many plastic drones; because all the internal parts are hidden, the drone appears neater and more professional. It can also offer additional weather protection.

Landing gears are similar to aircraft legs. These gears are frequently used on multirotors to prevent any equipment that is mounted on the lower part, such as video cameras, from collapsing when landing. Most landing gears are fixed, but retractable carriages can also be mounted. The majority of fixed-wing thrones do not use landing gears and instead land directly on the fuselage. Landing gears are only used for larger fixed-wing aircraft because most of them land on grass. If, however, an aircraft is landing on a more abrasive surface, it is advisable to add reinforcements to the lower part of the aircraft to ensure greater protection.

Yet another aspect to consider is the ground clearance offered by the landing gear, particularly when mounting equipment, such as video cameras, under the drone. If so, ensure that there is enough space to do so.

The size of the cart's contact area with the ground will be relevant depending on the type of landing surface that has been planned. For example, when landing on softer surfaces–snow is the most extreme example–some landing gears do not have sufficient ground contact area to keep the drone from sinking. Thus, many drone pilots add foam tubes to their carts to increase the contact surface.

3.2. The operation of drones

The autopilot can be considered the brain of the drone as it processes all the information and sends the necessary commands to the motors and control surfaces to perform the desired actions. Most autopilots include sensors such as gyroscopes, accelerometers, barometers, and a magnetometer, which are used to measure the motion of the model aircraft while in flight. The autopilot will use this information to keep the drone flying toward the set target, commanding the motors and other control surfaces. In the following paragraphs, we analyze the autopilot in detail.

When discussing the autopilot system, we refer to all its major components, including the control unit, external GPS sensors, and telemetry. The control unit is the main component of the system and performs all the calculations that are required to keep the drone in flight; however, it is not always capable of controlling the flight completely autonomously. In some cases, additional sensors such as the GPS are needed. Some control units have only essential sensors, such as an accelerometer and a gyroscope, because the other sensors are unnecessary and would only increase the cost of the unit. For platforms such as racing quadcopters, the control unit is only used to keep the aircraft stable while the pilot controls it, so additional sensors such as a barometer or the GPS are rarely used. These basic controllers are ideal in that they are less expensive and easier to set up because their primary purpose is to stabilize the aircraft rather than perform completely autonomous operations. Some control units also include an liquid crystal display and buttons, enabling the set up and configuration of the aircraft without a PC connection because everything is visible on the screen. The most advanced control units support multiple sensors, such as the GPS, and other accessories that enable far more advanced functions, such as the ability to take off and land independently or fly to specific waypoints and perform some actions automatically.

Such sensors are the most important sensors of the autopilot as they measure the aircraft's angle and rotation and keep it stable. Essentially, an accelerometer is a small device that measures gravity. Most modern accelerometer chips include three accelerometers for measuring the three axes (x, y, and z). The current angle of an aircraft can be calculated by combining the measurements of all three accelerometers. Similarly, gyroscopes measure acceleration or rotation, and, as with accelerometers, most gyroscopes can make three-axis measurements. Unfortunately, in real-world applications, sensors such as gyroscopes lose accuracy over time, and because accelerometer readings become distorted (owing to centrifugal forces) when an aircraft turns, it can be difficult to keep track of the true angle of the aircraft. The autopilot, however, is can estimate and correct errors. To obtain more accurate readings, some combine information from additional sensors such as a GPS, barometer, and compass. This process is known as "sensor fusion." The accelerometer and gyroscope, however, are essential to have on board to estimate the angle at an acceptable level while flying. When launching the autopilot for the first time, the accelerometers must be calibrated because the manufacturing and transport processes may have left them slightly unbalanced. Further, when turning on the drone, before flying, it is extremely important that it is not moving so that the accelerometer and gyroscope can be initialized as best as possible.

The barometer is a highly sensitive pressure sensor that is used on autopilot to measure the altitude of an aircraft. As the aircraft rises or falls, the air pressure changes, which corresponds to a specific change in altitude. Most barometers include a temperature sensor to compensate for pressure variations that are due to the temperature, and most of the barometers used on autopilots at present can measure subcentimeter variations in altitude reading.

Although pressure variations provide excellent indications of altitude variations, they are not always entirely accurate in detecting the absolute altitude of an aircraft in relation to sea level. Thus, the altitude information that is detected by the GPS is combined to obtain a better estimate; therefore, when taking off, the autopilot can use the altitude from the sea level recorded by the GPS as the calibration point and measure the small relative changes with the barometer.

The magnetometer, as with a normal compass, measures the magnetic field around an aircraft and informs the control unit of its orientation. Because a fixed-wing aircraft only flies forward, it is considerably easy to assess the direction, so compasses are primarily used for multirotors, which can fly at a fixed point.

Having a compass on board an aircraft that has motors with large magnets and other electrical wiring means entails substantial magnetic interference, which can cause problems with the sensor. Thus, the compass is often part of the GPS module and is mounted away from all other electronic components to minimize interference.

Because the magnetic field differs depending on the location, performing a quick compass calibration is crucial to obtain the best performance with a drone in new air.

GPS receivers are the devices that provide a drone with information regarding a location. The GPS functions by measuring the time that it takes for a signal sent from a GPS satellite to arrive at the receiver. Because these signals are distorted and sometimes bounce off other objects, they take longer to arrive; as a result, the GPS is not perfectly accurate: measurements are typically accurate to 5–10 m horizontally and approximately 15 m vertically. The most useful aspect of the GPS is that it provides an extremely accurate absolute three-dimensional position of the aircraft relative to the earth; by combining this data with that of other sensors such as the barometer, which measures relative height, it is possible to efficiently estimate the position of the drone. Being connected to more satellites will provide a better approximation of the drone's position. Prior to takeoff, the autopilot will wait to connect to a sufficient number of GPS satellites to record the initial position and save this takeoff position as a *home point*. Subsequently, if something goes wrong or if the drone requires reentry, it can land in the same spot or a few meters away (owing to the aforementioned GPS errors). In either case, being connected to more satellites will provide a better approximation of the drone's position, resulting in a greater reliability and accuracy.

Most autopilot systems include a *power module*, which is used to supply filtered and regulated energy directly from the battery to the controller. Because most electronics operate at 3.3 V or 5 V, the module will convert the battery voltage (which is usually much higher) to the 5 V that is required by the control unit.

The power module often includes a current and voltage sensor that measures how much energy is left in the battery, similar to a car's tank gauge. Some controllers can also estimate the remaining flight time and can automatically take control, return to the starting point, and land before the battery is completely discharged.

The addition of distance sensors improves the aircraft's functionality and safety. Most of the distance sensors used on drones are ultrasonic and determine the distance by measuring the time that an ultrasonic signal takes to bounce off an object. Other more expensive and accurate systems use lasers to measure the time that a light beam takes to bounce off an object. These laser-based systems also have a significantly higher operating range than ultrasonic sensors. The most common application of these sensors is to measure an aircraft's distance from the ground, which is particularly useful for landing or taking off. However, these sensors can also be mounted to look forward and prevent the aircraft from colliding with an obstacle. Ultrasonic sensors work best when flying over hard surfaces such as concrete because more natural materials such as grass can deflect and absorb sound impulses, consequently reducing their accuracy.

Almost all tones rely on GPS satellites to determine their location. However, when flying indoors, near tall buildings, or under large trees, the GPS signal is often too weak to obtain reliable positional information.

Consequently, some autopilots support the use of optical flow sensors to help automatically maintain the position of the aircraft, allowing the multirotor to autonomously maintain its position without the GPS.

An optical flow sensor is essentially the same type of sensor that is used on a computer mouse, that is, a low-resolution video camera that records the motion of the pixels that it sees to estimate their displacement.

However, optical flow sensors only work at low altitudes (less than approximately 10 m above the ground) and on surfaces with sufficient contrast, such as grass.

A fixed-wing drone can estimate its speed using the GPS module, but this only provides the ground speed (the distance traveled on the ground between two points in time). However, because there is often wind, the *airspeed* above the wings does not always correspond to the ground speed. The indicated airspeed, as measured by the sensors, differs slightly from the actual airspeed, which is affected by atmospheric conditions and altitude. Because the airspeed and the speed that is given by the GPS are considerably similar on calm days, many fixed-wing aircraft do not have an airspeed sensor.

However, having an airspeed sensor provides the autopilot with the real speed of the drone, which is important for preventing a stall. An airspeed sensor is a differential pressure sensor that uses a pitot tube, which protrudes from the front of the drone. The airspeed can be calculated by comparing the static and dynamic pressure values from the pipe.

On a multirotor, an airspeed sensor is unnecessary: the drone does not stall because the engines provide all the lift that is needed to keep it in flight.

Control units often have the ability to set different flight modes, which is useful because it allows for the drone's behavior to change during flight. Flight modes are usually controlled by the remote controller with one of the switches.

The actual mode changes depending on the control unit used, but the basic ones are as follows.

- Stable mode is the basic flight mode, often called the manual mode, which keeps the drone horizontal and stable. This mode should always be used for safety reasons in case something goes wrong.
- Stunt mode is a mode that is designed for stunts and makes the drone's response far more sensitive. The stunt mode frequently does not straighten the drone, instead keeping it in its current position to perform various aerobatic maneuvers.
- Altitude maintenance is a mode that is similar to the stunt mode; however, it also controls the altitude of the drone to make it fly at a specific altitude.
- Position hold is a mode that uses the GPS sensor to hold the drone in a defined position. Fixed-wing aircraft will circle the location, whereas multirotors will fly at a fixed point.
- Return to departure is a mode that, when activated, will fly the drone at a preset altitude before returning it to the takeoff position. Some controllers will control the drone to make it land where it started from. This flight mode is useful in an emergency or in the case that the drone is no longer visible.
- Automatic mode is a mode in which the autopilot will control and fly the drone. Usually, this involves setting a mission for the drone with waypoints, including automatic takeoff and landing. Some autopilots also allow you to perform certain actions, such as retracting the landing gear or taking a picture, at waypoints.

Some control units can record the data that are detected by the sensors, enabling post-flight checks (i.e., exactly the same purpose as the black box on a pilot aircraft). Many controllers store flight data on *secure digital* (SD) cards, while others rely on the internal memory. Recording data is an extremely useful feature, particularly during an accident or if something does not work properly, because it enables a detailed examination of the events and an identification of the cause of the problem or the accident. Some autopilots, such as the ArduPilot platform, also include PC software that automatically analyzes the flight log to detect the most common issues.

Vibrations, as with video cameras, can cause problems with the controller. Regardless of the platform used, it is always a good idea to mount the controller on an anti-vibration mount to ensure that the accelerometer and gyroscope do not have incorrect readings owing to the vibrations.

Every electronic device that controls a physical object has a negative feedback mechanism called the *proportional–integral–derivative* (PID) control. For example, if a sudden gust of wind causes the drone to rotate to one side, the PID control measures the difference between the actual roll angle and the desired one, which is zero. Based on this error, the PID control determines the most suitable command to send to the motors to straighten the quadcopter as soon as possible, without exaggerating or swinging around the horizontal position. PID controls are used for numerous aspects of the control unit, such as to maintain a preset altitude and to stay in a specific GPS position.

The proportional term will send a proportional correction to the error. Returning to the example of the quadcopter in the roll phase, the further that it is from the equilibrium position, the harder the motors will have to work to return to the horizontal. Having a P-term value that is too low will result in an unstable aircraft because the correction will never be enough to bring it back to the correct position. Increasing the P value changes the strength of the correction, making the quadcopter respond faster; however, if the P value is too high, the correction causes the drone to overtake the equilibrium position, making the drone tilt in the opposite direction. To reduce this excessive response, the value of P can be decreased, but this might make it too slow for the quadcopter to return to the horizontal position; thus, the *integral term* is introduced.

The integral term essentially controls the maximum correction that can be made to reduce excessive distances; it is based on the size of the error between the current position and the reference one. The integral term increases or decreases the correction based on how far it is from the reference point and how rapidly it changes.

The integral term can be thought of as a method to dynamically vary the term P according to the situation. In the case of a quadcopter that has become unbalanced by a gust of wind, the integral term will result in a strong correction signal being sent to the motors to begin straightening the quadcopter in the shortest time possible.

The derivative term controls the rate at which an aircraft returns to its reference position. The term D is not often used with most controls because setting the P and I values correctly will lead to an adequate performance. Setting a higher value for the derivative term will make the aircraft less responsive as the engines will be slower.

A ground station is not essential for the drone, but it completes the system, allowing for the parameters of the model to be monitored and changed while it is in flight or for a video to simply be viewed in real time. A ground station consists of all the equipment that is used on the ground for the unmanned aircraft.

The telemetry modules are radio devices that are connected to each other, enabling communication with the autopilot while it is in flight. Most telemetry systems allow communication in both directions; namely, information can be received from the autopilot, and commands can be sent from the ground. A simple telemetry system comprises two modules: one positioned on the aircraft and the other on the ground.

Ground station software is used to control the drone from the ground, while telemetry modules are used to send and receive commands between the ground station and the aircraft. Many autopilot systems include ground control software, which usually consists of some kind of map, so that the aircraft's progress can be tracked and waypoints can be set.

To operate at a greater distance with telemetry and the video transmission system, a high-gain antenna can be used. These antennas focus the signal but are extremely sensitive to direction; thus, if the antennas are not pointed directly at an aircraft, the signal is poor. Some pilots use a tracker antenna to solve this problem, which is a station with two servos that allow the antenna to rotate and tilt up or down so that it is always pointed toward the aircraft.

This system requires telemetry, which involves the transmission of the aircraft's position to the ground so that the antenna knows which direction to point in.

It should be noted that it is illegal in most of Europe to fly an aircraft without making eye contact; therefore, the use of tracker antennas is uncommon as it requires a special permit from the National Agency for Civil Aviation (ENAC) to fly a drone over long distances.

3.3. The radio control system

Although it is technically a drone that can fly autonomously, the remote control (often abbreviated to R/C or RC) is an important part of any APR system because it allows the user the ability to control the drone manually if needed. A radio control system consists of a transmitter (the device you hold in your hand) with levers and buttons that control the aircraft. When the levers are moved and the buttons are pressed, the transmitter sends the relevant radio signals to a receiver onboard the aircraft. These signals are read by the receiver and converted into commands for the autopilot, which then performs the required actions.

Here are some of the main features of the remote control.

When flying a drone, you normally hold a transmitter in your hands. Its two levers are used for the main control of the aircraft: managing the throttle, roll, pitch, and yaw. Other functions, such as the flaps and landing gear, and autopilot-related controls, such as changing flight modes and controlling the onboard camera, can be controlled via other buttons and switches.

The transmitters operate in two possible ways: mode 1 and mode 2.

Essentially, the modes define the functions of the main control levers. A simple method of distinguishing them visually is to look for the throttle lever, which is easily recognized because it does not have a spring that brings it back to the center as with the other levers. If the gas is on the left, the transmitter is most likely in mode 2; if it on the right, the transmitter is probably in mode 1. Mode 2 is the most common setting in which the throttle and yaw are controlled by the left lever, with the up and down movement controlling the throttle and the right/left movement controlling the yaw.

The right lever controls the roll and pitch, with pitch being controlled by vertical movement.

Mode 1 transmitters, in which the throttle/yaw and roll/pitch positions are reversed, are more common in the Far East.

When the term "channels" is used in relation to radio controls, it refers to the number of controls that the radio controls are capable of, namely, the outputs that are available to the radio system. Controls such as throttle, roll, pitch, and yaw each occupy a channel on the system. Typically, when flying a drone, at least these five channels are required so that four can be used to control each axis of the drone (roll, pitch, yaw, and throttle), while the last channel (usually a switch) is used to change the flight mode on the autopilot. However, having multiple channels is more common so that controls can be added to orient the camera, take a photo, or raise and lower the cart. Some R/C systems can even control multiple aspects with a single channel, allowing for *mixing*.

One of the most important steps to perform before takeoff is to ensure that each channel is set in the correct direction so that if the throttle is set to idle, the aircraft will recognize the signal in the same manner. Some aircraft can crash if this step is neglected before the first flight. Depending on the audio control system or autopilot being used, the R/C signals might be read slightly differently; consequently, all R/C transmitters have the ability to invert a channel.

The dual-rate and exponential parameters adjust the outputs in relation to the readings of the levers. Consider, for example, the roll lever (or aileron control) on the transmitter. With the default settings, it can be assumed that the neutral position with the lever in the center produces an output of 0. Moving completely to the left results in a −100% output, while moving completely to the right results in a +100% output. Thus, the output's response is linear in relation to the lever's input. Setting a dual rate to 50% means that the outputs are halved; if the lever is moved completely to the right, the output will be less than 50%. The dual rate is particularly useful with a fast fixed-wing aircraft. Because the movement that is needed on the control surfaces is reduced when flying faster, lowering the dual rate makes an aircraft less sensitive and easier to control as the control surfaces will only move 50% of their full extension.

Instead of using a linear relationship between the input of the lever and its output, an exponential function that is linked to the movement can be used to adjust it. Exponential shifts have the advantage of still offering the full range at the output, providing more control in the central region. Therefore, if the lever is moved completely to the right, an output of +100% is still present, but the output will be scaled so that when the lever is moved, say, by 25% to the right, the output will be reduced by around 10%. This enables more lever movements around the less sensitive center position, which is ideal for more aerobatic aircraft.

Mixing allows for multiple outputs to be controlled with a single channel.

In radio-controlled aerobatic aircraft, mixing is frequently used to combine flap and roll controls: by moving the roll lever to extreme positions, an aircraft's ailerons and flaps move simultaneously, allowing it to roll faster than it would if only the ailerons were being used.

Mixing is hardly ever used on multicopters because the control unit takes care of it.

A failsafe defines the behavior of an aircraft when it loses its connection with the remote control. Although rare, this might happen when the remote controller's batteries run out during flight or if the aircraft flies beyond the range of the remote controller.

Some remote controls can change the transmitter module by simply inserting a new one at the back.

Some modern equipment allows for telemetry information and control signals to be combined to monitor different parameters onboard the aircraft.

An R/C receiver is a small module that is mounted on the aircraft and receives command signals from the R/C transmitter. The R/C receiver is connected directly to the autopilot inputs, which also supply power to the receiver.

As with R/C transmitters, receivers have a specific number of channels, with each representing an output.

This does not mean that the receiver and transmitter must have exactly the same number of channels.

Binding is the process of connecting the R/C receiver to a specific transmitter.

When discussing an R/C receiver, the type of antenna must be considered because it indicates the strength and range of the connection. Most cheaper R/C systems use a single wire antenna, which results in a poor signal reception over longer distances.

Using two wires would constitute an improvement because this improves the antenna's ability to perceive signals.

Pulse-width modulation (PWM) and *pulse-position modulation* (PPM) refer to the methods by which the R/C signal is encoded.

PWM is the most common method for managing devices such as electronic speed controllers and servos. PWM requires a single cable per channel; thus, an eight-channel receiver will need eight connectors.

PPM can be thought of as aligning several PWM signals one after the other.

The most obvious difference is that a single cable can carry information on several channels through PPM; accordingly, an eight-channel receiver can be connected with a single connector.

Neither method is superior to the other; however, numerous drone manufacturers prefer PPM because it tends to lead to a cleaner and simpler connection.

3.4. Aircraft engines

The most commonly used motors for radio-controlled aircraft are brushless electric motors, which provide high power for low weight.

Simply put, a brushless motor comprises a stator (the fixed part) and a rotor (the rotating part).

The stator is composed of coils that are arranged radially, with copper cable rolled up on each coil to form electromagnets.

The rotor consists of magnets, which are arranged inside the external part of the motor.

To make the motor rotate, energy is applied to a specific set of windings at extremely precise intervals, which requires the use of an electronic controller to manage the speed of the motor.

An outrunner motor is the type that is used almost exclusively when it comes to electric multirotors or fixed-wing APRs. Outrunner motors have the rotating part on the outside, hence their name.

By contrast, an inrunner motor has a rotating part inside the engine.

Inrunner engines are most commonly used with radio-controlled cars.

In a brushless motor, patterns are identified by a series of four digits, which is sometimes followed by two more. These numbers define certain characteristics of the engine.

The first four digits give an indication of the physical dimensions of the engine (the first two indicate the diameter of the entire engine; the second two define the height of the entire engine).

The KV value represents the number of revolutions per minute of the motor per volt.

As can be expected, motors with a lower KV spin slower and motors with a higher KV spin faster.

A low KV motor is created using windings of thinner wires around each electromagnet.

The configuration number conveys how many electromagnets there are on the stator and the number of permanent magnets on the rotor.

Electronic speed controllers (ESCs) are devices that are used to control brushless motors.

A brushless ESC sends power to a motor at specific intervals, which makes the motor spin at the desired speed. The ESC sends signals to a certain section of the motor to activate the electromagnets at specific times, thereby causing it to rotate.

Everything is controlled by a small computer (called a microcontroller) that is placed inside each ESC. Note that when it comes to ESC sizing, we usually refer to its output in amperes rather than to its physical size.

Some ESCs have battery-eliminating circuits (BECs).

In practice, an ESC with a BEC is capable of delivering a constant voltage that can be used to power R/C devices, such as the receiver, servos, and controller. It is important to check the specifications of the BEC, which will often have a maximum output current. If the equipment uses more current than what the BEC can deliver, the drone will likely crash.

The two main types of firmware used for multicopters are SimonK and BLheli. Both began development by providing the year, but SimonK firmware was written for ESCs using Atmel microcontrollers, whereas BLheli was written for SiLabs microcontrollers.

All ESCs have a set of parameters that can be changed depending on the type of aircraft.

The most common method is to use the musical tone programming menu, which uses audio tones to change various parameters.

A slightly simpler method is to use an ESC programming card. This device can help set all the desired configurations and automatically load them onto the ESC in one step.

The last method is the USB connection, which essentially requires connecting the ESC to the computer to change settings via software (programming via software).

When the battery voltage drops, some ESCs stop sending power to the motor to save it for the remaining electronics, such as the R/C receiver, control unit, and servos.

When no throttle command is sent to the ESC, this setting causes the motor to stop rotating, applying force in the opposite direction.

Timing refers to the rate at which the ESC sends a current to each of the motor phases, causing the motor to spin.

It is typically set to 8 KHz or 12 KHz. Increasing this setting may cause the motor to run more efficiently, but the regulator will generate more heat because the current flowing through it changes considerably rapidly. The calibration process adjusts the ESC to the maximum range of input signal values and specifies how they should match the gas.

The calibration process simply shifts the throttle range of the regulator to match the inlet exactly such that when the throttle lever is at full throttle, so too is the regulator's outlet to the engine. The drone is controlled by the direction of the motors' rotation.

When you connect an ESC to a motor, it will rotate in a specific direction depending on the order of the cables. To reverse the motor if it turns in the wrong direction, simply swap the two outer cables.

3.5. The composition and type of propellers

The propellers create the thrust to drive the aircraft, thereby allowing it to fly.

A larger propeller can produce more thrust at a given rotational speed. When a propeller rotates slower, it is more efficient because the air has more time to stabilize as the propeller turns, and when it meets the leading edge, it is less turbulent.

The material is an important factor to consider as it determines the flexibility, cost, and strength of the propellers.

Plastic is the most commonly used material owing to its low cost. For propellers, various plastic compounds are used, ranging from nylon-based, which are the most flexible, to acrylonitrile butadiene styrene, which is somewhat stiffer. The main disadvantage is that plastic propellers are not as strong as other materials, making them unsuitable for lifting heavy loads.

Reinforced plastic propellers are a suitable compromise between plastic and carbon fiber because these propellers are sufficiently sturdy while still being cheap.

The added stiffness means that these propellers hold their shape better than plain plastic and are slightly more efficient.

These propellers are the most rigid because the carbon fiber is extremely strong and light. Their stiffness makes them the most aerodynamically efficient and suitable for heavier drones that generate more thrust.

Currently, wooden propellers are rare because of their cost and heaviness. For these precise reasons, wooden propellers are unsuitable for aerobatic multirotors. These propellers are sometimes mounted on drones that are used to make movies and have to lift heavy weights.

Foldable propellers have the ability to fold in flight or to be stowed away. This is particularly common on fixed-wing gliders that have an engine.

When at a high enough altitude, the engine can be turned off, and the propeller will fold back because of wind resistance, consequently becoming more aerodynamic.

On a multirotor, instead of folding backward, the propellers fold to the side for easier transport and storage.

The primary disadvantage of using folding propellers on a multi-rotor is that these propellers tend to be more expensive and heavier than stationary ones.

If using a drone for photography, this is a particularly important step because unbalanced propellers constitute the main cause of unwanted vibrations, which then result in blurry photos.

The balancing process minimizes vibrations by ensuring that both sides of a propeller have the exact same weight so that the center of gravity is located at the center of the propeller and motors.

A propeller balancer is essentially a shaft on which the propeller is mounted.

There are two steps to take when balancing a propeller:

• balancing the blades and
• balancing the central hub of the propeller.

3.6. Batteries

Batteries are used to power any component on the APR, including the engines, autopilot, and other devices.

The most commonly used batteries for drones are lithium polymer (LiPo) batteries, which have the highest energy density compared to other batteries, such as nickel–cadmium or nickel–metal hydride batteries.

LiPo batteries need special attention to last as long as possible and must be stored safely.

All batteries have two connectors: the main one, which is the one with the thickest cables, is the main power connector from which the energy is supplied. The second connector, which is smaller and has more cables, is known as a balance connector.

The C rating of a battery represents its discharge rate, in other words, the maximum amount of energy that can be obtained from a battery at any one time.

All batteries have a useful life in terms of the number of charge and discharge cycles.

LiPo batteries should never be stored when fully charged or fully discharged. Batteries should be stored with a 50%–70% charge.

3.7. Video and photo shooting tools

The choices of drones and cameras are interdependent as drones have limited carrying capacities.

The primary function of an first-person view (FPV) camera is to provide a real-time view from the drone's perspective. Typical FPV cameras are based on considerably small and light cameras that are used for security; their image quality is low when compared to the standard cameras found in stores.

Owing to this poor quality, FPV cameras are often only used for aircraft navigation, while a second camera with a higher quality (such as a GoPro) is used for high definition (HD) recording.

Since FPV cameras are used to fly an aircraft, they are mounted directly on the frame, with no gimbal for stabilization, so the pilot can see how the aircraft reacts when hit by gusts of wind.

FPV cameras have two types of sensors: *charged coupled devices* (CCDs) and *complementary metal oxide semiconductors* (CMOSs).

CMOS cameras are more expensive and heavier than CCDs but are typically better for FPV applications owing to their wide dynamic range and higher sensitivity to light.

Camcorders, such as the GoPro, are popular because they can record high-quality video with a small and light camera. GoPro cameras are popular for use on drones because these cameras can connect directly to the video transmitter, seeing what the camera sees in real time and, as a result, making it easier to know exactly what is being recorded.

Most gimbals are designed for GoPro cameras.

For professional applications such as mapping or aerial photography, small digital cameras or *digital single-lens reflex* cameras are often used because such cameras can take photos that have a higher quality.

Because the camera is mounted on a drone, pressing the shutter button to take a picture is obviously impossible. Consequently, a remote shutter control is used.

There are four main types of remote release systems:

- infrared, which is a method that uses an infrared LED (IR LED) that blinks in a particular pattern and at a certain rate that is detected by the infrared port on the camera;

- direct cable, which is another option as some cameras do not have an IR port and is a common with Canon cameras, where the camera can shoot when receiving a signal via a USB cable connected to the autopilot;
- mechanical, which requires a servo to be mounted on the camera that physically presses the shutter button; and
- timer, which is a method that can be used for some cameras that can repeatedly take pictures at set intervals wherein shooting can start by pressing the button when a drone is on the ground, after which the camera will continue to take pictures at set intervals while the drone is in flight.

The quality of the images that are captured by a drone can be affected by vibrations. Therefore, when mounting the camera, it is important to isolate it from vibration using a vibration-reducing stand or soft double-sided tape.

A gimbal is a device that keeps the camera stabilized while the drone moves through the air.

With the use of a small camera, wireless video transmission, and a monitor, FPV allows the remotely controlled aircraft to be flown virtually.

The other main use for FPV is video creation because having a wireless video transmission from the camera makes what is being recorded viewable, thereby making it far easier to acquire the perfect shot.

A basic FPV system consists of a camera that is connected to a video transmitter, which sends a wireless signal to a receiver on the ground.

An FPV transmitter is a device that wirelessly transmits images from the onboard camera to the ground, where the FPV video receiver will read the signals and display the images on a monitor.

The FPV video receiver is a device that reads the video signal from the transmitter and outputs a signal that can be read by the FPV monitor or viewer.

Some FPV receivers include a *digital video recorder* function, which lets FPV material be recorded on an SD card.

Some FPV receivers have a feature called diversity that enables the use of more than one antenna, where the receiver will automatically switch to the antenna that currently has a better signal. Diversity is an advantageous feature that allows the receiver to obtain a better video signal.

All FPV equipment includes a basic antenna; however, it can be replaced, if desired, with more suitable antennas that offer greater distances.

Directional antennas offer a far greater range in the direction toward which they are pointed, but the signal is not picked up outside the beam. Hence, directional antennas sacrifice amplitude for distance.

By contrast, omnidirectional antennas have a shorter range but have coverage within a spherical space.

When an antenna uses linear polarization, radio waves are generated in linear planes. Because the signals move along these linear planes, the best signal is received when the antennas on the transmitter and receiver are aligned. The disadvantage is that when an aircraft is in flight, the antennas do not remain precisely aligned, which can cause signal separation.

For this reason, circular polarized antennas are preferred.

Circularly polarized antennas radiate in a circular pattern. Their main advantage is that the signal is less dependent on the antennas on the transmitter and receiver being parallel since the signal emitted by the antenna is circular and does not travel in a single plane, such as in linear polarization.

Specifically, circularly polarized antennas are ideal because these antennas ensure a reliable signal even when steeply tilted.

It is often useful to overlay some flight-related information onto the video. This data may include an artificial horizon, the vehicle speed, the reentry direction, and battery information.

This is known as an on-screen display (OSD). Because the data shown are from onboard sensors, almost all OSD devices connect to the autopilot and video transmitter or are built into an autopilot system.

4. The applications and use of drones

1. Introduction

As is well known, the drone market is rapidly growing in terms of popularity, partly because of the various applications that are linked to it. Although it is not yet possible to affirm their widespread use, drones have now overcome some of the rigid and traditional barriers that have characterized various sectors over time and hampered the spread of technological innovation.

For some time now, drones have played an extremely important role in the operations of various companies and government organizations, infiltrating areas wherein some industries were stagnant or lagging behind. From making rapid deliveries during rush hours to scanning unreachable military bases, drones are proving extremely useful in situations where human operations have faltered against the needs of the market.

The achievement of higher efficiency and productivity targets, the reduction of labor costs, the increase in *customer satisfaction*, and the management of safety–as understood in its broadest meaning–are only some of the challenges that concern–on a global landscape–the industrial implementation of drone technology. As several studies (as mentioned below) have amply demonstrated, drones allow for remote locations to be reached while significantly reducing labor costs, thus requiring minimal expenditure for the organization in both operational and economic terms. These are, therefore, the real reasons for the adoption of drone technology in various commercial and, primarily, military sectors.

2. The public knowledge and acceptance of drones

The use of drones is constantly expanding; this is demonstrated by the various uses and applications that can be derived from drones for both military and civil purposes (refer to the following paragraphs). The theme, in this case, is understanding the perceptions of these aircraft among consumers, users, and nonusers. This aspect is of considerable importance because it is directly connected to the drone regulation process; it is impossible to develop strategies to effectively manage a drone revolution without an awareness of the public's awareness about drones.

Fig. 4.1. Public Awareness of Drone Applications

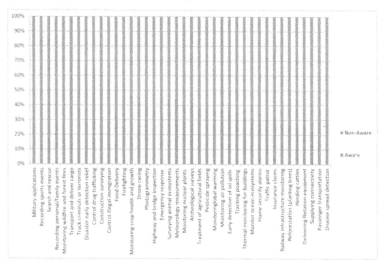

Source: Burchan Aydin (2019).

Several studies can be found in the literature in this regard. Tam (2011) addressed the issue of knowledge concerning drones, followed by a further study by Reddy and DeLaurentis (2016), who stated that 93% of the respondents who constituted the general public had heard about drones–mostly through traditional film and media–while users knew about the subject mainly from commercial literature or personal experience. The examination conducted in the aforementioned study therefore revealed that most of the interviewees were unaware of the technological limitations and history of drones, a factor that substantially influences the acceptance and perception of drones.

This concept was also highlighted by Eyerman (2013), who found that the public had a rather low level of awareness regarding drones, reaffirming the notion that an incomplete knowledge of a phenomenon influences its acceptability and perception by the general public. Thus, the regulation of the phenomenon should be promoted in parallel with information campaigns concerning the uses and risks that are associated with drones.

Fig. 4.2. Sources of Information for the General Public

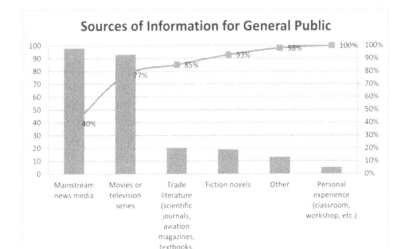

Source: Burchan Aydin (2019).

In this light, Russel (2016) highlighted that regulation, the clarity of application, and cultural misunderstandings about what drones can do comprised the main challenges for the quicker adoption of drones in different sectors. Further, Boucher (2015) aimed at examining the first association that people had when asked about drones and showed a different acceptance between their uses for social purposes and uses for private purposes (entertainment and hobbies). According to the results, applications for social purposes were well appreciated, whereas the public believed that applications for private purposes required careful monitoring and regulation.

In other words, there are several variables that influence a user's expectations, including the correct information regarding the use of drone technology; moreover, the conception of a specific theme evidently differs from area to area depending on the principles and concepts that characterize a territory. Mac-Sween (2003) stated that the public acceptance of drone freight transport increased by 15% (from 37% to 52%) when the public was given educational information. Moreover, some investigations concluded that the public perception of drones depended on where they were used and for what purposes. The results of a nationwide survey also showed that the majority of those surveyed were opposed to the private use of drones for purposes such as deliveries, aerial photography for weddings, or other recreational events but supported the use of drones for social activities such as safety inspections, aerial photography for terrain mapping, and wildlife monitoring. This is because the public associates a positive relationship between the benefits of and the risks linked to certain applications such as search and rescue, terrorist monitoring, and crime prevention. By contrast, applications with private purposes do not obtain as much consent because such applications are directly connected to personal issues such as those of privacy and security.

Given the aforementioned studies, it is clear that public perception depends on the specific application of drones. However, if the associated risks are mitigated by adopting effectively publicized strategies, the public acceptance of drones could be achieved in the near future. Nevertheless, at the moment, drones are primarily viewed as aircraft with security and privacy risks, and the genuine advantages of their applications remain underappreciated. In this sense, given the rapid advancement of these tools in recent years, it would be appropriate to mitigate this aspect by better communicating the associated benefits and risks of drones.

3. The application of drones

As noted in the previous chapters, although the development and use of drones on a global scale can be traced back to the last two decades, their true origins can be found in the First World War when France and the US launched a project to develop automatic and unmanned airplanes.

Over the last two decades, more attention has been paid to drone technology, which has increasingly prospered because of the different applications thereof, ranging from the military sector to logistics, transportation, security, and even agriculture (Rodriguez et al., 2013). In addition to its uses in the military sector–a sector that has always been a proponent of technological innovations–the development of technology in the commercial and personal fields is also notable. In commercial terms, few companies are currently committed to developing routine technologies and business functions using drones, although important investments have been made by industrial conglomerates, chip companies, and IT consulting firms. Drones, which are becoming more sophisticated and complex, are expected to aid industrial activities in various sectors by performing tasks such as detecting places that are difficult to locate or reach, monitoring road accidents, and engaging in tasks that are related to precision agriculture. If, however, there is a certain fervor for the introduction of drones into the industrial sector and for their commercialization, concerns regarding all aspects that relate to safety increase; the massive marketing of drones, even for personal use, undoubtedly requires a clearly defined regulatory system, which raises the question of a possible limit to the expansion of this technology.

One of the main safety concerns is with respect to the invasion of sensitive airspaces, such as airports (Boselli et al., 2017), power plants (Solodov et al., 2018), and personal environments (Daly, 2017; Aydin, 2019). Furthermore, recent studies have raised critical issues regarding the ethics of using drones for surveillance purposes (West & Bowman, 2016) as well as in relation to amenities, such as the impact of noise (Chang & Li, 2018).

In these terms, the issue of public acceptance comes to mind. In reality, although several steps forward in terms of regulation remain to be taken following the demilitarization of drones, the growing attention of the media has gradually increased user trust and acceptance (Freeman & Freeland, 2016). Consider the impact that drones have had on public perception as a result of innovations in the delivery of food and medicines to homes, environmental interventions, civil and environmental safety, and, generally, an increase in supply within numerous commercial sectors.

To examine the different applications of drone technology, it is first necessary to investigate how these applications can be classified. Hassanalian (2017) offered a representation of the different areas in which drones are used, ranging from rescue missions to environmental protection, postal shipping, delivery activities, and other diverse applications (Yan et al., 2010).

Fig. 4.3. Type of Applications

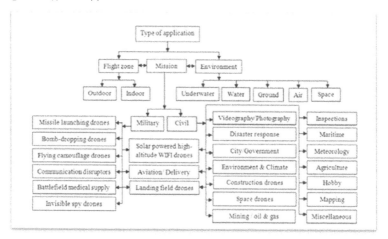

Source: Own elaboration.

The use of drones in various areas is characterized by the need for the specific characteristics of these objects, such as the ability to provide an aerial overview of the target area and the speed of execution; the latter is variable and sometimes plays a primary role in achieving the goal.

Generally, drones have multipurpose uses in both civil and military fields. The main uses are illustrated below.

3.1. Military applications

Drones have played a fundamental role in military strategies, particularly in intelligence and reconnaissance activities; they are used for a variety of purposes, ranging from protecting ground troops via Persistent Close Air Support (P-CAS)/precision strikes to anticipating a potential air attack via laser-guided missiles (Pirnie et al., 2005) and precision shelling against terrorist targets (Callam et al., 2010). Drones can also provide guidance and air support in covert operations, such as by carrying out surveillance, target acquisition, and reconnaissance; reconnaissance, surveillance, and target acquisition; and/or combat, intelligence, surveillance, and reconnaissance.

The following figure shows some examples of drone applications in the military and security fields.

Fig. 4.4. Examples of Drone Applications in a Military Industry

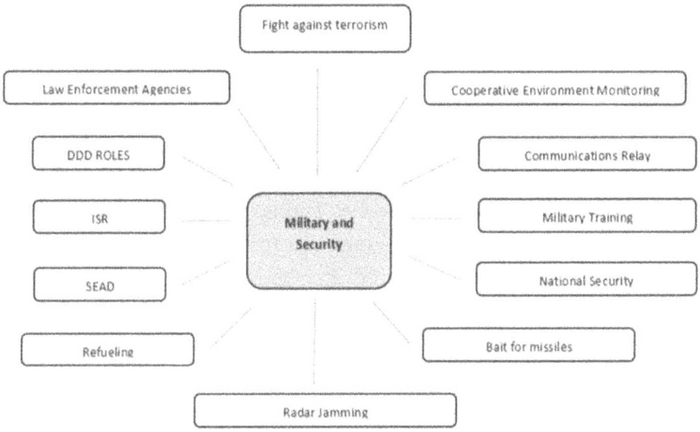

Fight against terrorism

Law Enforcement Agencies

Cooperative Environment Monitoring

DDD ROLES

Communications Relay

ISR

Military and Security

Military Training

SEAD

National Security

Refueling

Bait for missiles

Radar Jamming

Source: Own elaboration.

√ **Dangerous rules**: when surveying heavily protected areas, the loss of a UAV is less compared to the loss of an aircraft with people on board. In these missions, stealth UAVs that are hardly detectable by radar are used, which become difficult targets for missiles and anti-aircraft fire. During these operations, the crew's concentration can be compromised by various factors, such as stress, tension, and/or too many flight hours. Using such aircraft enables the avoidance of diplomatic incidents and derogatory television political propaganda that can be generated by, for example, capturing pilots.

√ **Dirty rules**: these rules involve both military and civil applications, such as monitoring the environment after nuclear or chemical contamination to avoid endangering human lives.

√ **Dull rules**: long hours of observation and surveillance (without interruption) by trained subjects can lead to fatigue and a loss of concentration, which can affect the outcome of a mission and the achievement of the given objectives. A UAV that is equipped with HD color video, data transmission, thermal imaging cameras, and radar scans can perform such tasks more efficiently, at a lower cost, and without the aforementioned human limitations.

√ **Law enforcement agencies:** many police departments have used drones to maintain public order by conducting aerial surveillance. Since 2005, US Customs and Border Protection has used UAVs with the intention of using armed drones. In 2013, the FBI stated that it owns and uses UAVs for surveillance purposes. Similarly, in 2014, five British police forces reported using UAVs for surveillance. In August 2013, the Italian defense company Selex ES built an unarmed surveillance drone for the Democratic Republic of the Congo that aimed at monitoring the movements of armed groups in the region to protect the civilian population more effectively.

√ **Fight against terrorism:** ever since the US entered the war to fight terrorism, the difficulty in fighting an irregular and asymmetrical war has been recognized. In this sense, the use of drones has been considered the most effective way of fighting asymmetrical war threats [and] conducting rapid and destructive operations in order to paralyze the enemy.

√ **Cooperative environmental monitoring.**

√ **Military training targets:** since 1997, the US military has used over 80 F-4 Phantoms, which have been converted into robotic aircraft for use as aerial targets.

√ **Protection against other UAVs:** the US has developed defense systems against low-level drone attacks. Two German companies have developed 40 kW lasers against UAVs. Other British companies have jointly developed a system to monitor and halt the control mechanism for small UAVs.

√ **Territorial security–borders and the fight against drug traffickers:** in 2011, the US began a collaboration with Mexico to stem the phenomenon of illegal immigration and drug trafficking across the border. The drones involved in this collaboration fly approximately 18,000 meters high, are practically invisible from the ground, and can meticulously cover an area of around 100,000 km² in a single day.

√ **Convoys protections.**

√ **Reconnaissance and surveillance.**

√ **Coverage roles.**

√ **Research roles:** some UAVs are used for research and development in the aeronautical field for testing purposes. In these cases, UAVs are designed to scale, both in the military and civilian fields, to carry out more realistic, less expensive, and less dangerous tests. Based on the results of the tests, changes are made to the real models.

3.2. Civilian applications

Gradually, the use of drones has also evolved to play an important role in the civil field. From an analysis of the academic literature, several applications stand out that can be divided into four main categories: monitoring/inspection and data acquisition, photography, logistics (including passengers), and recreation.

3.2.1. Monitoring, inspection, and data collection

As seen in the previous chapters, drones have enabled new methods of information and data retrieval at considerably lower costs and with higher collection capacities than other tools. The use of these tools allows for real-time analyses to be performed and detailed information reports that go beyond the capabilities of operational control teams. Some of the main uses that have emerged in recent years relate to precision agriculture, mining operations, and even data collection regarding industrial construction sites. The agricultural sector uses drones to acquire more precise information on the degree of hydration of the soil or to identify crop health problems to plan timely irrigation times and areas as well as effective applications of fertilizers and pesticides (Na et al., 2017). Similarly, drones have been employed in mining operations to monitor ore stocks and bleeding reliefs for maintenance issues as well as to analyze the following: explosive ore prior to its processing (Bamford et al., 2017), access to water bodies in hazardous/remote locations to facilitate sampling for environmental management (Langhammer et al., 2018), and imaging mines for rehabilitation (Moudry et al., 2019).

It is clear that the development of more efficient methodologies generates positive externalities in terms of both the environment and the economy. In general, drones have become reliable and efficient tools in recent years owing to notable advances in aerospace technology, avionics, and image sensors and represent a new solution for *earth observation* that is positioned in a complementary manner between traditional remote sensing platforms and ground detection instruments.

As mentioned earlier, however, drones are also used in other contexts, including on construction sites and in seismic emergencies in the context of safety and technical interventions. In numerous cases, such as when natural or artificial heritage has been damaged by natural disasters, monitoring and intervention actions must be performed on buildings and the like to guarantee the maximum safety possible for the operators. Understandably, carrying out urgent technical interventions during seismic emergencies turns out to be a considerably different activity from planning ordinary building sites and involves additional risks for the safety of the operators. The use of drones in this sector, combined with the improvements in geomatics systems as well as photogrammetry software allows for the accurate and cost-effective documentation of the conditions of environmental and building heritage.

Over time, the acquisition of data and information from above through increasingly sophisticated and economical instruments, as a means of support for a decision-making process, has manifested, from a commercial perspective, interests and applications that have gradually extended into other sectors such as photography and the image–in the broadest sense. The use of images for mere aesthetic value has witnessed, in recent years, an increasing use of drones, both for personal use, such as documenting a private event like a wedding, and for commercial use, such as during sporting events or marketing campaigns.

As noted previously, the various uses represent an extension of this equipment into recreational spaces, which are also associated with entertainment. This is due, in part, to the increased public awareness of drone technology, which translates into a greater familiarity with it and a broader consideration of its potential applications.

Therefore, we are witnessing an increasingly transversal use of drones.

3.2.2. Logistics and drone operations

In recent years, because of impressive technological advancements, drones have seen a significant increase in use in the logistics sector owing to their low cost, small size, and programmable features. Currently, UAVs can perform inventory, transport cargo by air, and conduct security tasks. In particular, sustainable delivery appears to be one of the main challenges that companies intend to face in the logistics sector, with drones interpreted as an economic and ecological response to business needs. Despite the lack of a perfectly defined regulatory and legal context, the main players in the logistics sector now agree that delivery by drones represents a primary challenge of the future.

Several examples demonstrate the intense experimentation activity in this regard. In 2019, Amazon introduced the MK27, a new drone that appears to be more efficient, reliable, stable, and safer than previous models in the drone fleet. MK27 uses AI to operate autonomously in its environment and can detect people, animals, etc., and make appropriate maneuvers in response (Snow, 2019).

Fig. 4.5. Amazon Prime Air

Source: www.amazon.com.

In addition, also in 2019, Wing, the start-up Alphabet's drone delivery company, in partnership with FedEx, Walgreens, and a local retailer, made its first delivery in Virginia. In Australia, Wing proposed a service with which home delivery, using drones, food, and healthcare products from pharmacies booked through a mobile app, becoming the first American airline approved by the FAA in April 2019. Furthermore, Dronamics, the air freight start-up, proposed the Black Swan model, which aims to democratize air transport and reduce shipping costs in emerging markets; a new type of unmanned aircraft has been developed that can be monitored and managed remotely via satellite, with which it is now possible to transport 350 kilograms over 2,500 kilometers for a cost that is less than 50% compared to other airplanes.

In the warehouse sector, the invention by Geodis in partnership with Delta Drone is particularly notable as it was created by means of a battery-powered robot in combination with a quadcopter drone that is equipped with four HD cameras and controlled by geolocation.

There are also numerous projects that include trials for social causes, including one that allows the transportation of drugs to remote areas. One such project, carried out by DHL in 2018, involved the rapid delivery of sanitary products by drones in the remote area of Lake Victoria, Tanzania. UPS Flight Forward accomplished the same in North Carolina; in October 2019, the same company announced that it was partnering with CVS Pharmacy to develop a variety of drone delivery use cases.

Further challenges in the logistics field include, for example, the delivery of heavy equipment that necessitate vertical takeoffs and landings; these cases are particularly relevant for deliveries that are made on ships at sea, shipyards, etc. In this regard, one example is the experimentation of the Autonomous Pod Transport 70 (ATP 70) 3 or the drone developed by Volans-i-a start-up based in San Francisco–that is capable of carrying up to 90 kilograms of payload at a speed of 320 kilometers per hour, using electric batteries for low-energy vertical take-offs and landings.

Fig. 4.6. APT 70

Source: https://www.forbes.com/sites/erictegler/2020/10/02/bell-learned-that-its-apt
   -70-cargo-drone-can-integrate-with-manned-traffic-during-a-demo-flight-what-did
   -it-learn-about-avoidance-and-5g/?sh=4e040b852e1f.

The analysis of these cases focuses on the different approaches that companies adopt to create new solutions for the logistics sector, ranging from warehouse operations to last-mile delivery drones and unmanned cargo aircraft.

3.2.2.1. *Drone–truck combined operations (DTCO)*

The use of drones for logistical purposes has increasingly attracted the attention of researchers and professionals. Excluding large drones, which are generally used for military purposes, the combined use of drones and trucks is currently being tested–a phenomenon that has advantages and disadvantages. Although drones can travel at high speeds, are certainly faster than trucks, and do not have to follow predefined road routes, drones are far more limited in terms of load capacity and travel autonomy compared to trucks.

The aforementioned aspects can be addressed in part by using the two vehicles in tandem; combined DTCO comprise a system in which a drone and a truck work together to perform object delivery/collection, reconnaissance, inspection, monitoring, etc. This issue has recently attracted the attention of numerous companies, such as UPS, which tested its truck–drone delivery system in 2017.

In general, a drone can leave a truck, deliver or collect a package, and return to the truck without any human intervention while the truck simultaneously delivers additional items to customers by acting as a mobile hub for drones. Once the drone returns to the truck, its battery can be easily replaced so that it is ready for the next trip.

There are several critical issues concerning the DTCO with respect to the delivery of items (through routing for a set of positions), area coverage, scheduling, the assignment of tasks, and the location of the facility. In this sense, one of the most crucial issue involves the synchronization between the drone and the truck, which is directly related to the efficiency of the operation. Depending on the application areas, such a synchronization is required, for example, to refuel the drone with items that need to be delivered, to replace or charge a drone battery, or to perform drone maintenance or repair. If this synchronization is required, the vehicles must arrive at a predetermined position at the same time; alternatively, one vehicle must wait for the other at a predetermined position without leaving this position.

Moreover, when drones and trucks function as synchronized work units, their roles are generally equally important. A drone can take off from a truck, deliver an item to a customer, and then return to the truck to recharge/replace a battery so that it is prepared for the next delivery. Simultaneously, the truck also delivers an item to a customer as it moves to the next location at which both vehicles can meet.

In the case of a single drone and truck, such a scenario can be formulated as the *"flying side-kick traveling salesman problem"* (FSTSP) (Murray & Chu, 2015) or the *"traveling salesman problem with [a] drone where the concept of operation is used"* (TSP-D) (Ha et al., 2018). In these formulations, FSTSP uses the concept of sorties, whereas TSP-D employs the concept of operations. The synchronization constraints in these models dictate that the drone and truck arrive at the interchange at the same time. Synchronization is a critical problem because it is difficult to achieve. If the vehicles do not operate in unison, there will be inefficiencies in both economic and operational terms.

It is clear, however, that such issues occur only when the recipients are outside the drone's range of action; if all the customers are within the drone's flight range, namely, within a range of action that guarantees the drone's autonomy, the need for the drone to land on a truck would be negated because the drone could return to the deposit to replace/charge its batteries and acquire another item to be delivered. Simultaneously, regardless of the operations of drones, trucks can deliver items to customers. In this case, the objective is to minimize the makespan by researching the optimal tour of a single truck and determining the number of drones to be used in consideration of the fact that drones, as with trucks, can be used in the delivery or in the collection phase.

Drone as a primary and truck as a supporting working unit

Drones can play a major role in the majority of the activities considered thus far, such as construction monitoring, chemical spraying in agriculture, the delivery of items in logistics, and disaster management research. These services could be considerably enhanced in terms of performance if drones could land on support trucks or service hubs to, for example, recharge/replace batteries, refuel products faster, and travel a certain distance together with the supporting vehicle to save energy. In this regard, the literature has proposed a model called the "vehicle-routing problem with drones" (Wang & Sheu, 2019), which provides a service hub to which trucks deliver products while drones deliver items to customers. This model assumes the existence of multiple drones that are limited in terms of range and flight capabilities; the model is characterized by the fact that the drones are only expected to land on hubs rather than on trucks. The objective, in this case, is to minimize the cost of the trip as a result of the combination of the fixed cost of the truck and the cost of the drone and truck trip.

Truck as a primary and drone as a supporting working unit

Regarding the problem of delivery, the routes of the truck (mobile carrier) are sometimes planned by assuming an additional delivery by drones; this is a situation wherein the truck plays a main role with respect to the drone. The drones, which are launched from the truck that is following its (predetermined) path, aim to reach as many customers as possible depending on their capacity before returning to the truck. One interesting variant of this problem, in which the truck is replaced by an air vehicle or a ship, is called the "*mothership and drone routing problem*" (Poikonen, 2019). This model considers the path of two vehicles that are traveling in tandem. The largest vehicle, which can be a ship or an airplane, is called a "mothership," whereas the smallest vehicle, which can be a small boat or a drone, is called a "drone." This solution is crucial for activities such as search and rescue and deliveries to island locations.

Barriers to the implementation of the DTCO

Despite the recent increase in interest in the DTCO, several implications currently hinder the adoption of this operating model. These barriers can be classified into two macrocategories: regulation (e.g., privacy and security) and sustainability (e.g., the environment, technology, and socio-economy).

Fig. 4.7. Barriers to the Implementation of the DTCO

• Main criteria	• Instances
1. Privacy	• Surveillance against privacy related legislation
	• Mass data collection
2. Security	• Data security
	• Cyber-physical attacks
	• Identification of non-authorized drones
3. Safety	• Regulatory concerns to the general public
	• Risk of accidents
	• Air space safety
4. Environment	• Wildlife disruption
	• CO_2 emissions
	• Pollution (noise, visual, etc)
5. Technology	• Performance (flight range, battery life, routing network, carrying capacity, weather Flight control (air collision, obstacle avoidance)
	• Countering advesary threats
6. Socio-economics	• Economy and employment
	• Public perception and acceptance

Source: Aydin (2019).

As previously stated, drones can be viewed as a serious threat to privacy because of the emergence of problems related to their functionality (e.g., the retrieval of data or images from private places) as well as problems related to the presence of an as-yet undefined regulatory regulation. One issue regarding the security of the collected data is clearly connected to this as the data could be sold or leaked without authorization, thereby creating serious problems that relate to civil liberties.

Drone safety issues are also generally associated with security issues because drone control can be subject to malfunction or hacking, resulting in accidents such as falls on the ground or collisions in the air. The proliferation of drones can further complicate the issue because an increase in the number of drones in the air affects not only the likelihood of these accidents but also the nature of the causes. Many have speculated that flight altitudes should vary depending on the type of drone; however, collisions could also occur during take-offs or landings.

Furthermore, the increased use of drones could cause environmental issues, such as flora damage and CO_2 emissions, as well as have a negative visual and aural impact, leading to the phenomenon known as "full skies." This last point contradicts the general belief that using drones for deliveries is more environmentally friendly than using conventional trucks because it has been demonstrated that drones, particularly when used over long distances, emit more pollution than trucks.

The adoption of these solutions is also subject to barriers of a purely technological nature, which are clearly connected with those noted previously. In operational terms, for instance, the adoption of these solutions is related to the flight range, battery life, and load capacity of drones, which are aspects that inevitably mark a boundary of use, even in economic terms.

Finally, there is the socioeconomic aspect, which is connected to the fear of repercussions in terms of employment and social fabric given potential problems such as mass unemployment or a polarized economy. However, while technological advancements reduce the need for certain professional skills, such advancements also create new job opportunities that require different qualifications and tasks.

This leads us to believe that the adoption of similar technologies must begin with agreements among the various economic stakeholders involved, with an adequate consideration and interpretation of the potential consequences of such an adoption.

3.2.3. Drone applications during the COVID-19 pandemic

The COVID-19 pandemic will most likely be remembered as a watershed moment for the widespread use of drones. From medical deliveries to monitoring and remote inspections, fleets of drones have made it possible in some cases to overcome economic and health problems at a time when people can be both the victims and sources of the spread of an infection.

Technological advances in robotics have enabled companies to develop new systems for order preparation, inventory management, and order delivery. Drones have now become genuine working tools in the logistics sector and have been recognized to play an important role in the delivery of goods.

Despite several issues concerning weight and volume, the reduction in delivery times enabled substantial benefits during the SARS-COV-2 pandemic when there was a high demand for healthcare products. One area in which the need to reduce delivery times has been felt most is in the distribution of drugs and medical supplies in affluent areas as well as the transportation of tests to diagnostic laboratories and drugs to individual homes. Undoubtedly, during an emergency such as that of COVID-19, robotics, AI, and engineering can play a decisive role. In a context wherein patients are no longer placed in a single center but are rather in their own homes, the problem not only concerns the organization of assistance but also involves the planning of care shifts as well as the delivery of drugs and care equipment.

In general, drones have been shown to constitute a valuable tool to help improve the quality of services, especially in health emergency situations. This is because the applications of drones could be appreciated: the mapping of areas, the delivery of essential products in remote or difficult-to-access locations, and the ability to assess the damage by retrieving aerial information–activities that aid the health sector during a pandemic.

UAVs are increasing the availability of medicines in rural and remote areas around the world. Frequently, UAVs constitute the best method of sending a product in the shortest amount of time, especially when road transport is too time-consuming. Consider how, during a pandemic, providing diagnostic laboratories with patient samples as soon as possible is essential because this allows doctors to ascertain the diagnosis and make decisions in a timely manner.

Nevertheless, privacy concerns remain; in particular, at the Italian level, an emphasis was placed on an authorization issued by the ENAC that gave the green light to the use of drones in derogation for monitoring citizens' movements in some municipal areas, with the aim of ensuring the containment of the epidemiological emergency. This measure has been criticized for its violation of privacy as it allowed private institutions and bodies to acquire images and data during inspection flights.

Thus, the issue of maintaining the correct balance between the right to health and the right to privacy emerges. Although the priority of public health is undeniable and was a condition that influenced the ENAC's provision, the right to privacy as an expression of personal freedom cannot be denied. Therefore, it appears necessary, in this case and as repeatedly stressed before, to establish a regulatory process of intervention that, while pursuing the objective of containing an epidemiological spread, does not justify an uncontrolled prejudice to other fundamental rights, including those of privacy and confidentiality.

4. The market dynamics of drones for civilian use

The previous chapters have demonstrated how the drone market is rapidly expanding and characterized by high technological dynamism. However, barriers remain to the implementation of drone technology, with respect to autonomy, to the processing capacity in relation to weight, and, most importantly, to a regulatory system that has yet to be fully defined.

The regulatory aspect also assumes considerable importance in light of the differences in regulations across countries, which can act as a deterrent to investments by leading companies in their sectors. Existing regulations are mostly deficient and vary greatly from country to country. This is true in almost all conceivable market segments for commercial RPAS market segments, albeit to varying degrees.

The main distinction is safety for those who are uninvolved in the flight operation. In this sense, it must be considered that the market follows (and influences) the regulation, which makes it possible to foresee development stages and technological diffusion according to the contexts in which UAVs must operate.

From a contextual perspective, the sectors of agriculture (precision and nonprecision), environmental data collection, and infrastructure inspection and monitoring are evidently the most mature. The spread of commercial UAVs in these segments could lead to two fundamental benefits for further development:

– wider acceptance by the general public and
– the birth of professional figures who are specialized in one or more phases of the drone life cycle (flight, data analysis, maintenance, construction, etc.).

However, an important step for such development involves interpreting the dynamics of the market correctly. In this regard, the following considerations can be made.

– Although drone hardware technology is undergoing notable changes that characterize its general performance and specific features, the importance of hardware is diminishing compared to software, which will serve as a source of real differentiation.
– There is an increasing interest in the usability and use of drones; the drone market is turning to an inexperienced and increasingly large audience; thus, only companies that can implement solutions that are more suitable for a less tech-savvy public will be able to obtain the market's approval.
– In relation to data security and privacy issues, to date, the limited diffusion of technology has not necessitated anything more than sporadic attention to the data processed in and out of UAVs. However, as commercial segments develop, the data collected and processed by drones will become more commercial in nature. In short, drones will hold and process the sensitive data of customers who will have to deal with the companies that will use said drones. Moreover, remote or autonomous flight control is managed through a continuous exchange of information that en-

ters and exits an aircraft's flight controller, which lends itself to illegal cyber attacks.

– This final point is crucial for segments such as monitoring, urban infrastructure, short- and long-distance freight transport, and the transportation of people. These sectors, by nature, require a constant exchange of data, making them extremely vulnerable if not adequately protected by a suitable IT infrastructure.

Although various applications are being tested in the various sectors, these factors cause delays in the adoption of drone technology that can be partly attributed to the lack of investments by companies, which are intimidated by the implied competition with subjects that have been engaged in safety, manned air traffic management, and logistics for years. Thus, companies with more influence from consolidated military or security experience (such as Thales, Insitu, and Airbus) or with the financial strength to support extensive research and development (such as Amazon) will likely be key players.

From this perspective, the market for commercial drones seems to be divided into three main segments based on the complexity of the missions to be completed. The first segment, which is already maturing, is characterized by sufficient regulation, fairly strong technology diffusion, and customers who can demand an economic return for their investments in drone fleets. This market will increasingly comprise fairly standard hardware products as well as software solutions that are not necessarily closed and are subject to more or less invasive customizations.

The second segment is characterized by issues concerning social acceptance and, consequently, by the need to define an increasingly limited regulatory system. The operations required by drones in this segment will be far more complex, posing safety risks for both the aircraft and the people involved. The customers will be fewer (such as considerably large companies or institutional entities), but the requested products will have such unique characteristics as to be considered premium: nonstandard hardware products that will be sold together with highly customized software for the specific customer as well as a set of ancillary services cover the UAVs' entire life cycle. In this segment, the companies most associated with the military sector or innovation in a specific context will emerge.

Furthermore, by focusing on the supply chain, a third market segment aimed at manufacturing companies in the sector can be identified. This is the OEM (Original Equipment Manufacturer) market, which includes the components that are required for quad-copter technology in general. Depending on the dynamics of this market and the technology involved, the companies that operate therein will have to opt either for pricing strategies if the technology becomes so common as to be standard or for differentiation if the technology plays a critical role in the aircraft's performance.

5. Digital transformation and corporate communication

SUMMARY: 1. Communication in the value chain. – 2. The new forms of communication: methods and timing. – 3. Communication applied to innovation: the drone "case".

1. Communication in the value chain

In a scenario wherein a company is characterized by continuous transformations that are dictated by the development of digital technological innovation, corporate communication, or business communication, presents aspects of evident interest in its many manifestations.

Given that communication is a component of innovation, the strategic function of communication within an organization takes on new significance. The communication of innovation cannot be separated from innovation itself, which must make the results of its application known, shared, and usable to those for whom these results are intended to best express its potential.

After all, communication is a more complex phenomenon than what is imagined or perceived, and it has two minimal yet essential characteristics in its basic constitutive aspects. The first characteristic demonstrates how communication has a dual nature and physiognomy: on one level, it takes concrete form in a physical fact and material perceived by our senses (e.g. via writing, voices, images, or electromagnetic waves). On a second level, these communicative phenomena have value as tools that lead to the conveyed meaning, which is subject to the recipient's interpretation. The second characteristic of communication is that it is never confined to a personal phenomenon (i.e., a single subject) but always implies a relationship between several parts–a real exchange that happens in interpersonal or symbolic relationships, as in the case of mass media.

An essential element of the current challenge–where companies must respond to the changes that have been imposed by the Fourth Industrial Revolution and adapt to new operating conditions–lies precisely in communication as a continuous interchange of data (understood in a general and not a purely numerical sense). These are profound changes that require, now more than ever, an efficient use of information flows in the two major areas of communication intervention: within a business organization itself as well as without. Consider the need to convey accurate communication so that the various figures who operate within the company at various levels can adequately access information and thus process said information for production purposes.

It is therefore necessary to understand how the new communication paradigms are configured in relation to innovation; in essence, this is a matter of delving into those aspects that allow us to better understand how innovation is communicated and how it changes the forms and methods of communication.

Generally, corporate communication continues to represent a managerial tool through which a company addresses the relevant public to achieve various goals in a synthesis of various forms of expression. In this manner, the value of the company is transferred to and perceived by the recipients of the business. Within a circuit logic in which the drivers are always represented by defining what to communicate, to whom, and when, technological innovation disrupts the references of "how" to communicate, that is, through which tools and languages. Moreover, "knowing how to do" is insufficient for the company structure: it is also necessary to "let people know" and to "know how to represent and argue" (Pastore & Vernuccio, 2016) so that the value can be transmitted to the relevant public and therefore perceived and increased through communication, which is, as noted, a process of continuous internal and external interchange.

Similarly, a company's ability to bring innovation to the market and, in many cases, to stimulate the development of a new market (Simone et al., 2021) is heavily reliant on the effectiveness of its communication. Company stakeholders must be informed about the impact of AI on changes to the business model and about the consequences thereof. The innovations of the business models that are developed through the use of AI can lead to an increase in the value of the company for shareholders and offer new opportunities to various target audiences, including the customers themselves. The communications that the customers of a company engage in to suggest ideas and highlight what they dislike about an offer and/or current processes can also result in the innovation of a product, a process, or a system of actions within the corporate structure. In this sense, the availability of an active two-way communication channel with customers as well as with other target audiences can lead to the innovation or evolution of the business model, thus contributing to the creation of value. Because AI technologies evolve extremely rapidly, it is the communication agents who must inform and educate stakeholders about the impact of AI in business processes.

For the production dynamics of a company, innovation does not solely refer to conceiving, designing, and launching a new product or service on the market or defining a new business process; rather, it is essential for the innovation itself to be accompanied by actions that allow it to be perceived as a bearer of "value" by customers and stakeholders. The essential objective of the communication of innovation, when in reference to a "new" service/product/process, is precisely to explain the innovation itself in terms of its value, advantages, usefulness, functionality, and methods of adoption.

Moreover, corporate reputation is understood as a shared representation of the company's history and past results, describing its ability to generate economic and social value for its various stakeholders.

Although the cultural and social media and references of the issuers and recipients involved in the actions of corporate communication can change, the objective of such communication remains to spread and create value for the company itself, expanding its existing targets and conquering new ones. The spread of innovation is closely related to the effectiveness of the related communication. Effective communication entails conveying the correct message to the recipient so that it can be easily understood and remembered.

Digital communication takes place through the use of infrastructures and technologies that have a high potential for communication exchange and the following characteristics.

- **Interactivity.** The subjects of a communication, the sender and the receiver, often in a many-to-many model, can create a continuous flow of information regardless of the location and time of a message. Essentially, the subjects can be in contact with anyone at any time regardless of where or how they are.

- **Multimedia.** The establishment of a digital communication channel between the protagonists of a communication allows them to exchange and share messages in various formats: from images to videos, from voices to GIFs, and from messages to documents in various formats.

- **Hypertextuality.** This is the potentially infinite ability to access texts and electronic material on the internet as a result of having accessed the web. In its most obvious form, hypertext is manifested in the possibility offered by words or other content on the network (images, videos, etc.) to be "clickable" and to thus allow access to additional content of the same or different kind.

- **Immediacy.** Following an initial access to the reference technology, the real-time mode of action allows digital communication to modify, expand, and manage its contents at any time.

- **Horizontality.** The reference here is to the creative moment, to the source of communication, and to diffusion itself. The possibility of accessing technological tools that are universally available to any subject determines the ability of the same to enter any type of information into the communication circuit, often without initial control and selection. It is this "game" that, for example, increases the appeal of social networks while raising major concerns about the truthfulness of the news, the reliability of the sources, the limitations in terms of control over and access to communication tools, and, last but not least, the substantial issues of privacy and cyber security.

These elements, which form the basis of digital communication, represent the strengths that enable a company to reach its interlocutors in real time through diversified methods and provide them with cognitive tools to ensure an adequate and constant exchange of information with the corporate body. Numerous touch points, or points of contact, between the company and its interlocutors necessitate continuous attention and monitoring in terms of the information and communication flows that emanate from the company, which, as previously noted, contribute to the diffusion and creation of value.

Similar to how the multiplication of information channels that are available to citizens, which is favored by technological innovation, does not lead to disinformation, as demagogic attempts indicate, but rather makes citizens, even the youngest ones, closer and more attentive to information flows, digital innovation, by introducing communication tools with a high level of multimedia, represents an extraordinary resource that allows a company to realize the ancient "dream" of continuous contact with customers.

Communication thus becomes an essential driver for value creation in the context of the interaction between a company and its target audiences.

This includes the so-called customer experience, which is an innovative approach concerning the customer. Companies can generate and increase value and profit as well as strengthen relationships with the recipients of their communicative actions through specific activities that provide, at various levels, sensory involvement for their customers and other target audiences. These are experiential elements that can not only lead to investments in a brand or product/service but also involve the material aspect and the physical or virtual spaces that are available to the business structure to create an emotional and social bond between the users and the product or the brand itself in an autonomous or coordinated manner. The products themselves are no longer communicated; rather, the emotions that the products elicit are conveyed.

In this manner, companies satisfy the digital customer's need for "engagement," which is the ability of a brand or product to create solid and lasting relationships with its users, establishing a deep bond and emotional value with customers. This occurs through the use of continuous, direct, contextualized, and personalized experiential activities that are carried out through various communication channels.

2. The new forms of communication: methods and timing

Communication that results from "digital transformation" can therefore be understood as the set of all activities that involve the creation and dissemination of content (texts, images, videos, etc.) through the use of digital technologies and tools such as PCs, tablets, smartphones, and satellites (Guidi, 2017). This affects companies' integrated communication strategies and actions, such as by involving the various levels of a company's structure. To effectively ascertain the potential inherent in this new communicative environment that characterizes innovative digital tools, particularly social media, it is sufficient to highlight how social media, in addition to offering a measure of the results of their actions, represent a tool through which a customer (and not only the customer) can extend their experiential contact with a company and with a product to the point of transforming the customer themselves into an active participant in the process of creating or changing the product. Moreover, continuous interaction enables companies to collect data and information that can be used to guide future decision-making processes (Masini, Pasquini, & Segreto, 2017).

The most important digital communication channels for a company are represented by the following.

- **Website.** The website of a company is its online interface, its showcase, and the business card with which its business structure expresses its values, communicates its position to potential customers, and provides institutional information to its target audiences.
- **Social networks.** A company gains online visibility and creates brand awareness through social networks. These networks constitute the heart of digital communication, which comprises various communication channels. The most commonly used ones are now well known, from Facebook to Twitter, Instagram to LinkedIn, WhatsApp to Pinterest, and so on.
- **Video marketing and YouTube.** YouTube's video sharing and archiving platform is the most widely used "video marketing" tool at present and is essentially configured as a video search engine, within which a company can activate its own channel.
- **Blogs.** A blog is a web space wherein users of various types (companies, organizations, individuals, etc.) publish content in the form of a diary, with the possibility of interaction between users and the author(s) of a given blog.

- **Mobiles.** This tool includes all the communication activities integrated with mobile devices, particularly smartphones and tablets. Mobile-first, or conceptualizing a message that is best suited for a mobile, is one of the new "mantras" of digital communication.
- **Forums and newsgroups.** These comprise discussion and comparison groups, often of a monothematic nature, that are generally hosted on specific sites and platforms.

The presence of an effective digital communication control enables a company to move toward the new actions that are taken by consumers and is identified by the new marketing model as the zero moment of truth (ZMOT). As theorized by Google's Jim Lecinski in 2001, the ZMOT is understood as the moment in which a consumer, after receiving a stimulus for a purchase, goes online to search for information and decides whether, when, and where to buy a product or service (Lecinski has expressed his concepts in an e-book that is easily available on the internet). In essence, before purchasing any type of good or service, consumers naturally search for information online using electronic devices, often smartphones. This is the result of the digital age that has transformed the purchasing process. Before the digital age, the purchasing process consisted of three phases. Consumers first perceived a need (natural or induced) to buy a good or service and then went to the store and proceeded to choose the good on the shelf in what was called the "moment of truth." The third phase involved the consumption of this good. In the new consumption model, however, after the customer has confirmed their purchase need but before the moment of truth (the shelf), there is an intermediate step: a search for information regarding the good or service to be bought, or the ZMOT. To be effective, a company must be prepared to provide answers and indications at this stage, and digital platforms play a central role in this regard. For a company, this entails being present and accessible on various devices with the appropriate messages.

Faced with a new paradigm that is dictated by digital transformation and changes in customer purchasing behavior, communication as a corporate strategic function responds by fully using the tools that have been made available by technological innovation.

However, this activity is guided and planned by the definition of a new communication system, which takes the form of specific methods of use and interaction with the different channels available. The following modes of expression can be applied for the communicative function.

- **Transmedial mode.** In this mode, a company communicates its contents through multiple media, each of which can integrate new and distinct information. The purpose of transmedial communication is to invite a customer (or a potential customer) to enter your world to allow them to know you or to share company content on social media. Accordingly, the customer becomes a communicator to the point of conveying company products and services on their own social profiles.
- **Cross-media mode.** This mode comprises the creation and distribution of content that is connected on various social platforms as well as the monitoring of said content to ensure its effectiveness. The cross-media approach involves the possible connection of different means of communication with each other via digital platforms. In this case, the strategic advantage derives from the possibility of obtaining media interaction. More than any other element, the communication that is linked to the customer experience induces one to think in cross-media terms, where one cannot reason and act for a single communication channel alone. Rather, the entire communication must be conceptualized as a single narrative that is then redesigned in the various "tones of voice" that are suitable for each communication channel.
- **Multichannel mode.** In a multichannel mode, a company conveys its messages to a substantial number of people at the same time or at different times through an integrated system of means. The aim of increasing communicative effectiveness is thus pursued.
- **Integrated mode.** Integrated communication uses all communication tools, online and offline, through a shared and coordinated image: the tools are exploited in an associated and effective manner to have a strong impact on the target audience. The communication channels, not only digital but also traditional (including the so-called "above the line" channels, such as television, radio,

press, and billposting, and "below the line" ones, such as promotions, sponsorships, and public relations), to choose from are numerous, and their effectiveness depends on the final purpose and the target audience (Poggiani & Pratesi, 2016).

These functional aspects of communication are the result of the proliferation of touch points between a company and the concerned public owing to technological innovation. With respect to the customer, a collaborative and participatory purchasing process occurs that compensates for the persuasive effectiveness of one-way communications, which essentially belong to the traditional forms of corporate communication that are essentially resolved through the use of mass media (the television, the radio, newspapers, billboards, etc.).

Among the elements that are used to amplify the effectiveness of digital communication is storytelling, which consists of building and telling a story to arouse the interest and attention of the target audience, with the aim of convincing them to take a specific action.

The scientific literature that analyzes the new business dynamics that have been generated by the Fourth Industrial Revolution essentially configures three different guidelines for the modification of corporate communication.

- A director is based on the **adaptation of communication methods**, which are critical elements that influence the dynamics of a company's internal and external communication. The director intends to strengthen relationships at all levels of the company as well as with partners by leveraging new technologies and increasing trust and transparency.
- A second director is focused on **analyzing the transformation of the selected areas of corporate communication**, including the reorganization of the system of networks and channels to be used in various corporate areas, with respect to the simplification of communication processes and flows as well as the storage and security of data.
- A guiding trend is centered on the identification and analysis of the new communicative actions that are generated by technological innovation.

The advancement of digital technologies has resulted in a shift in communication strategies. Retaining customers has become the primary objective of enterprises; thus, customer acquisition has taken a backseat to customer loyalty over the years. It has also become essential for an organization to be transparent–and therefore authentic–in its communication to build trust with its customers and maintain long-term relationships (Costabile, 2001).

Traditional marketing, after all, aims to establish an interaction with the consumer, whereas digital marketing seeks to consolidate a relationship with the customer, involve the customer, and thus produce results.

Currently, customers are connected, directly or indirectly, to the digital universe at any time and in any place. The "digital customer" has evolved from an initial consumer who is neutral, uninformed, and passive to a "prosumer" who is a more active customer and is connected to the network. The internet, therefore, offers the latter the opportunity to seek information and become more aware about their purchases.

Thus, traditional communication methods are now no longer sufficient. It is necessary to innovate because a lack of modernization is the most important factor that determines a company's loss of competitiveness. In addition, messages and languages must be differentiated according to the phase of adoption of the innovation in the market and for different customer clusters. Therefore, the engagement and call-to-action capacity of innovation communication are essential.

Communication channels can exponentially amplify the diffusion of innovation; however, if the message and medium are inadequate, the risk is that innovation will fail even if it is useful and valuable and has been heavily invested in the conception, design, and execution phases.

3. Communication applied to innovation: the drone "case"

The professional use of drones is peremptorily going beyond the boundaries of the areas of interest to which it was originally relegated, that is, from the application of photographic and video surveys, often in a hobbyist key, to an object of interest in new areas and areas of work that originally were not contemplated. By doing so, the case of drones comprises a constantly expanding phenomenon from a technological viewpoint. With the opening of new markets as well as research and investment horizons, communication regarding the various technologies that are applied to drones and their various applications is becoming increasingly important. This is, moreover, an essential way to enable the results of new research in the technological field to find effective channels of application for industrial and business purposes. Through communicative actions, the activities that are related to the technological evolution of drones and its related applications in various areas can leave the laboratory and share the results and benefits for the product or service, the market, and society with the relevant public. Innovative and potentially strategic products, such as the drone–given its numerous services and areas of application, as with many other technologies on the market today–necessitate well-researched communication that can immediately transmit the potential of such products and the related services.

Furthermore, as noted previously, among the essential purposes attributed today to communication is that of generating and disseminating value for a company and creating new targets that are connected to those of the customers on which the company is primarily focused, that is, the customers who are directly linked to the company's core product or service. The countless application areas and continuous technological developments have allowed drone manufacturers to strongly differentiate their target buyers, who can range from simple hobbyists to large multinationals. Communication then becomes decisive in pinpointing all the potential consumers given that the possible future strategic developments of the product/service in question, when linked to the use of drones in their various areas of application, are truly enormous in scope.

These findings are readily apparent when some aspects of the Communication Plan that was developed by an Italian company with the objective of externally communicating the innovative services of the drones that it has developed are examined. Communicative actions that aimed at raising the awareness of the target toward the new services and their various possible applications were thus studied. These actions fall within the scope of "corporate communication" and are therefore considered consistent with the messages that were issued by the entire business organization.

The Communication Plan, which was designed to be an effective tool for the scientific and structured development of the communication of results that relate to the creation of new products and services, enables one to plan and manage the communicative actions that are to be implemented to achieve specific corporate strategic objectives over a specified period of time.

The development follows an organizational process that is divided into three distinct phases:

- planning and editing, namely, the phase in which the plan is drafted;
- implementation, that is, the phase of a concrete realization and the management of the same; and
- evaluation, namely, the phase of verification of the results that have been obtained, of the impact and effects that have been generated, and of any discrepancies between these and the objectives that were set.

Regarding our concrete case as a reference, the characteristics of the drone market at an international level were highlighted, with a particular emphasis on the services that the drones themselves can offer. In this case, the service that a company intends to launch on the market consists of a platform for the analysis of the data that are collected by a drone, which includes hardware and software solutions for the detection, classification, and analysis of remote data, even in real time, by drones through the use of enabling technologies such as the cloud and Big Data analysis. The project uses the support of a drone that is equipped with technological equipment for remote detection (such as a camera and sensors), which, when flying over agricultural land, can send real-time data for a predictive analysis of the state of health of the crops present on the land. In addition to the agricultural sector, this service can be used in various other areas of intervention. The international drone market trends indicate that the services that can be provided by this aircraft have a high growth potential in the coming years. In this context, an effective communicative action is required to raise awareness of a new service and highlight its potential and benefits.

The communication strategy that was identified in the implementation of the Communication Plan, with the related techniques and tools responding to the needs of the company, considered a series of constraints and feasibility criteria, such as the available economic resources, the human resources within the company, the specific target audiences, and the available technological tools.

Subsequently, appropriate stylistic choices were made in conveying the messages to the target audience, with a selection or mixture of the different possibilities. Once all the architecture within which the Communication Plan was to be conveyed had been defined, the values and information that were to be transmitted in the construction of the messages in a coherent manner had to be prepared with respect to the objectives, audiences, and strategic choices that were carried out.

The communication tools are numerous and were selected by evaluating their consistency with the contents that were developed and the audiences that had to be reached on the basis of a dialogue to be built and consolidated with the latter. The considerations that were related to the presence of a technological service with a high added value, as in the case of the platform in question, made the use of a **cross-media communication strategy** particularly evident and effective. This strategy involves the combined and simultaneous use of different tools in which communication must be understood and managed as a narrative unicum. Therefore, the various messages must be communicated and modulated with different tones of voice depending on the particular characteristics of each individual communication channel. The cross-media communication paradigm has several strengths that can be leveraged, including the ability to make this type of communication less invasive and repetitive and more stimulating.

To ensure the effectiveness of the communication activity that related to the launch of the new services of the company in question and the use of drones, the organization of one or more events represents a valid tool for consideration. The perception of the value that an event can generate for the organizations and people involved in it in various capacities and forms has also been amplified because of the increased dissemination and visibility that new media offer, particularly in terms of the web and social networks. The ability to make the results and effects of such an activity usable through the communication platforms that are integrated with social media makes eventing one of the most productive forms in the planning of communicative actions.

The Communication Plan designed for the web platform for the management of services that are related to the drone envisaged a first step in the operational phase that was divided into two parts. The first part concerned specific issues regarding the application of the new drone on which to build short communication campaigns; the other part involved the commission and creation of a web platform. Subsequently, in the second step, all communication concerning the new product, its various applications, and technological implementations is primarily conveyed by the aforementioned platform and is integrated, supported, and enhanced by the other communication tools, thus creating an effective integrated communication system.

Conclusions

The analyses presented in the previous chapters that were conducted based on the existing literature highlight an interesting picture regarding the changes taking place in companies following intense technological innovation. The Fourth Industrial Revolution affects the human resources of a company in terms of roles and skills in addition affecting the value chain and the ways in which production is organized. Consequently, to improve production efficiency and product quality, new business models must be designed to systematize the opportunities that are offered by Industry 4.0 and allow companies to capitalize on innovation to gain a competitive advantage.

Owing to the benefit offered by 5G technology, which leads to the simplification of communications between devices, thus resulting in a considerable use in applications that are related to the IoT, the core of innovation that is linked to Industry 4.0 lies in the real-time availability of diverse information through the integration of all the elements of the value chain and the continuous monitoring of the parameters that are linked to these essential elements. For example, consider the case of the use of "*data mining*" techniques, namely, "data extraction," the process through which companies extract value from data on market prospects and, more simply, on the life cycle of a machine or a product. This creates the conditions for the design and implementation of innovative and customized products and services; however, at the same time, new challenges and criticalities are encountered.

Along with the creation of new services that add value to the customer experience (demand-pull), the Industry 4.0 paradigm, which is primarily concerned with adding value to the manufacturing process (technology-push), is considered the most recent trend that is capable of transforming businesses, particularly industrial ones. Indeed, the two aforementioned trends are in many cases complementary and necessarily lead to business model innovation.

One challenge, which is simultaneously a critical component, is the role that company personnel, the human factor, must play in the context of business planning and the new business models implemented by companies in an Industry 4.0 perspective. In this regard, a recent study published in the *International Journal of Production Economics* ("Industry 4.0 and the human factor: A systems framework and analysis methodology for successful development") highlighted how the Fourth Industrial Revolution is changing the role of the human factor (HF) in company operating systems but noted that HF remains an essential part of this operation. The study, therefore, emphasizes that a successful digital transformation must consider HF to avoid the pitfalls of innovation that is carried out without regard for this aspect, which remains widely underestimated in the research on technologies and implementation related to Industry. 4.0 Adequate systematic consideration and attention to HF in the digital transformation of work, the aforementioned research continues, can avoid negative consequences for individual employees, the organization of production, and for the company as a whole. Thus, incorporating HF can help overcome the challenges of the digital transformation of work. The spread of COVID-19 has increased awareness regarding the importance of business organizations' ability to keep up with digital innovations. Therefore, the regeneration of business models is becoming an increasingly crucial factor for survival in the digital age.

Traditional methods of conducting business have changed dramatically with the emergence of new digital technologies. Companies can remain competitive by using the advantages of the same technologies, such as the IoT, social computing, cloud computing, CPS, Big Data, wireless networks, AI, robotics, and simulations. This is highlighted by, among others, a special investigation (Technology in Society, February 2021) that proposed a process for the regeneration of the business model based on digital innovations. The proposed model, demonstrated with a real-world case study, demonstrates how strategic managers can use it to analyze the effects of potential digital innovations on their current business models up to the regeneration of the model itself. Therefore, it can help companies gain a competitive advantage over their competitors or support their businesses in terms of technological development.

In addition, yet another study (Technological Forecasting and Social Change, Volume 161, December 2020) highlighted that the Fourth Industrial Revolution offers a precious opportunity to drive technological innovation in the business environment and increase its productivity; however, this process also leads to a significant shortening of product life cycles, requiring an acceleration of the pace of innovation. However, relying solely on internal resources will prevent a company from accelerating the pace of its innovation. Thus, businesses are increasingly adopting an open innovation strategy that includes collaboration with external stakeholders. The crucial challenge that companies must face in the management of open innovation is the trust between the interested parties, which is understood as the ability to integrate and interact. Digital integration–as achieved through Industry 4.0 technologies and a company's ability to invest in digitization and new technologies–can play a fundamental role in this regard, and the aforementioned research specifically examines the relationship of the impact of digital transformation on open innovation activities. The data reported in the study concern 324 international cases of electrical and electronic companies in three major countries in the Asia-Pacific area: Malaysia, Indonesia, and Thailand. The results showed that technologies that were enabled by the Industry 4.0 paradigm had a significantly positive impact on a company's open innovation activity.

As detailed earlier, the changes necessary for companies in the Fourth Industrial Revolution find particular interests in terms of application in certain sectors, such as the logistics field. In this context, this publication has highlighted how modifying the production paradigm inevitably impacts logistics. Companies are receiving requests for ever-faster deliveries and increasingly sophisticated services, and logistics must evolve to adapt to the changing needs of the consumer and to the new rhythms of the company's production process.

4.0 technologies (IoT, Big Data, AI, augmented reality, and autonomous vehicles) can be applied in internal logistics to control the flows of materials, in warehouse management, and in distribution logistics. This perspective leads us to the field of drones. In addition to covering a wide range of services, drones are destined to take over some of the deliveries currently made by courier, for the infamous "last mile," making the drone an appealing investment in terms of hardware and intelligent solutions.

Other sectors in which the use of drones seems to be of great interest include environmental monitoring. In this field, three-dimensional surveys of the territory can be performed with drones to detect hydrogeological risk and for activities related to the agri-food sector. In addition, the applications of drones are notable in the industrial and civil sectors, where UAVs have become indispensable owing to their versatility and relative economic advantages. By using drones, companies can perform inspections concerning precision as well as continuous, timely, and immediate monitoring. This is all the more valid for areas that are difficult to reach or are located in dangerous contexts.

Alongside the considerable development of the use of drones in the civil and industrial sectors, with the market prospects of absolute value in the current decade also in reference to the services that are connected to the activities carried out with the use of drones, critical issues arise that might represent obstacles to the commercial use of remotely piloted aircraft. There are two essential aspects that can affect the market in question. The first concerns the protection of privacy and the confidentiality of data that can be acquired through the use of drones. Here, we enter a legal framework that involves the regulations governing the sector of remotely piloted aircraft, with the countries of the European Union seeking legislative uniformity and the need to regulate a sector that still presents issues that deserve to be explored in depth. This leads us to the second aspect: the issue of authorizations to guarantee the safety of the skies and the correct use of drones. As is well known, the potential and ductility of these increasingly sophisticated devices make them instruments that can be used in activities that might jeopardize the safety of citizens as well as industrial and military structures. The major world players in the logistics and transport sector have long understood the extraordinary possibilities of drones for carrying out commercial activities; however, the social and institutional contexts of their applications also deserve attention. This is the case for the use of drones for civil protection and rescue activities in inaccessible areas or at the service of medical and health facilities, which was tested in relation to the urgent delivery of medicines in the first phase of the COVID-19 emergency, with undeniably satisfactory results.

However, innovation as applied to business dynamics, considered independently, is not an element that can enable a company to acquire the necessary competitive advantage or, in any case, adapt to market dynamics. Innovation must be accompanied, as highlighted herein, by a change in the business model; moreover, innovation must also be adequately communicated to the relevant public. The introduction of new technologies in business processes is configured as an articulated process in which communication increasingly becomes a strategic resource and finds its functional application through the available and increasingly intrusive technologies, allowing for the diffusion of contents that are themselves innovative in terms of languages and tools. In this sense, the ability of communication to operate in a digital environment, such as by enabling the overlapping of languages, formats, and media, can help make communication relevant to a fluid and complex reality. The same Big Data that technology makes available to a company implies fundamental changes in how information is managed in the field of corporate communication as well as in the improvement of production processes and data-based business models.

One fundamental role in conveying the internal and external communication flows of a company is played by social channels such as Facebook, Twitter, Instagram, and LinkedIn, which can also be used by the company as a real point of contact for listening to the customer. Through interactions with the users of these direct communication channels, companies can understand the opinions that are expressed by the customers about specific issues and contexts, study trends and evaluate the reputation of products and companies, and anticipate phenomena and trends to the point of improving or replacing a product or service. Thus, communication, when supported by effective interaction based on social networks, can perform a predictive function regarding the planning of future business choices, often at a strategic level. Innovation is measured not only by the amount of technical innovation but also its impact on the market, and the diffusion of new products is always linked to the ability of consumers to understand their value in use and to acquire the logistics and operating methods through communication flows of which the consumers themselves are recipients and can intercept.

Moreover, the true innovator is not the one who has the ideas or owns the techniques but the one who translates them into concrete and useful facts and, above all, disseminates them. In other words, the true innovator can communicate them in an appropriate manner.

References

Ayala, N., Ghezzi, A., Frank, A. J., Mendes, G. (2019). Servitization and Industry 4.0 convergence in the digital transformation of product firms: A business model innovation perspective. *Technological Forecasting and Social Change*, 141(April), 341–351.

Aydin, B. (2019). Public acceptance of drones: Knowledge, attitudes, and practice. *Technology in Society*, 59, 101180.

Bamford, T., Esmaeili, K., Schoellig, A. P. (2017). A real-time analysis of post-blast rock fragmentation using UAV technology. *International Journal of Mining, Reclamation and Environment*, 31(6), 439–456.

Barile, S., Saviano, M., Polese, F., & Di Nauta, P. (2012). Reflections on service systems boundaries: A viable systems perspective. The case of the London Borough of Sutton. *European Management Journal*, 30, 451–465.

Basso B., Sartori L., Bertocco M., & Oliviero G. (2003). Evaluation of variable depth tillage: Economic aspects and simulation of long term effects on soil organic matter and soil physical properties. *Proceedings of the 4th European Conference on Precision Agriculture*, Berlino, 15–18 June 2003.

Borfecchia, F., Pollino, M., De Cecco, L., Lugari, A., Martini, S., La Porta, L., … & Pascale, C. (2010). Active and passive remote sensing for supporting the evaluation of the urban seismic vulnerability. *Italian Journal of Remote Sensing*, 42(3), 129–141.

Boselli, C., Danis, J., McQueen, S., Breger, A., Jiang, T., Looze, D. and Ni, D. (2017), "Geo-fencing to secure airport perimeter against sUAS", *International Journal of Intelligent Unmanned Systems*, Vol. 5 No. 4, pp. 102–116.

Boucher, P. (2016). You wouldn't have your granny using them: Drawing boundaries between acceptable and unacceptable applications of civil drones. *Science and Engineering Ethics*, 22, 1391–1418.

Callam, A. (2010). Drone wars: Armed unmanned aerial vehicles. *International Affairs Review, 18*(3).

Campbell, J. B., & Wynne, R. H. (2011). *Introduction to remote sensing.* Guilford Press.

Carta tematica della flora e della vegetazione delle montagne della duchessa. http://www.riservaduchessa.it/ctflora1.htm.

Cervelli, G., Pira, S., & Trivelli, L. (2017). *Industria 4.0 senza slogan.* Pisa.

Chang, S. J., & Li, K. W. (2018, April). Visual and hearing detection capabilities to discriminate whether a UAV invade a campus airspace. In *5th International Conference on Industrial Engineering and Applications (ICIEA)* (pp. 146–149). IEEE Publications.

Chen, C. H., & Ho, P. G. P. (2008). Statistical pattern recognition in remote sensing. *Pattern Recognition, 41*(9), 2731–2741.

Coskun, A., & Tanrikulu A. (2021). Digital innovations-driven business model regeneration: A process model. *Technology in Society, 46* (February).

Costabile, M. (2001). *Il capitale relazionale.* McGraw-Hill.

Daly, A. (2017). Privacy in automation: An appraisal of the emerging Australian approach. *Computer Law and Security Review, 33*(6), 836–846.

Dore, N., & Patruno, J. (2012). Le nuove frontiere dell'archeologia dalla fotografia aerea al telerilevamento satellitare sar. *Archeomatica, 2*(4).

Eyerman, J., Letterman, C., Pitts, W., Holloway, J., Hinkle, K., Schanzer, D., Ladd, K., Mitchell, S., & Kaydos-Daniels S. C. (2013). *Unmanned aircraft and the human element: Public perceptions and first responder concerns.* Institute for Homeland Security Solutions.

Faraz, M., & Petraite, M. (2020). Industry 4.0 technologies, digital trust and technological orientation: What matters in open innovation? *Technological Forecasting and Social Change, 161m* (December).

Forte, M. (1995). Scientific visualisation and archaeological landscape: The case study of a terramara, Italy. In G. Lock, & Z. Stanèiè (Eds.), *Archaeology and geographical information systems* (pp. 231–238). Taylor & Francis.

Forte, M., & Campana, S. (2001). Telerilevamento e paesaggi archeologici tridimensionali. *Remote Sensing in Archaeology*, 95–141.

Freeman, P. K., & Freeland, R. S. (2016). Media framing the reception of unmanned aerial vehicles in the United States of America. *Technology in Society*, 44, 23–29.

Fussell, J., Rundquist, D., & Harrington, J. A. (1986). On defining remote sensing. *Photogrammetric Engineering and Remote Sensing*, 52(9), 1507–1511.

Gao, J., & Liu, Y. (2001). Applications of remote sensing, GIS and GPS in glaciology: A review. *Progress in Physical Geography*, 25(4), 520–540.

Giacinto, G., Roli, F., & Bruzzone, L. (2000). Combination of neural and statistical algorithms for supervised classification of remote-sensing images. *Pattern Recognition Letters*, 21(5), 385–397.

Giardino, M. J. (2011). A history of NASA remote sensing contributions to archaeology. *Journal of Archaeological Science*, 38(9), 2003–2009.

Glock, C., Grosse, H. E., Neumann, P. W., & Winkelhaus, S. (2021). Industry 4.0 and the human factor–A systems framework and analysis methodology for successful development. *Journal of Production Economics*, 233 (February).

Godwin, R. J., & Miller, P. C. H. (2003). A review of the technologies for mapping within-field variability. *Biosystems Engineering*, 84(4), 393–407.

Golinelli, G. M. (2011). *Viable systems approach (VSA): Governing business dynamics.* Cedam.

Guidi, S. Comunicazione digitale. Mini guida per non sbagliare. www.digital-coach.it/blog/case-histories/comunicazione-digitale.

Ha, Q. M., Deville, Y., Pham, Q. D., & Hà, M. H. (2018). On the min-cost traveling salesman problem with drone. *Transportation Research Part C*, 86, 597–621.

Hassanalian, M., & Abdelkefi, A. (2017), Classifications, applications, and design challenges of drones: A review. *Progress in Aerospace Sciences*, 91, 99–131.

Huang, Y., Chen, Z. X., Tao, Y. U., Huang, X. Z., & Gu, X. F. (2018). Agricultural remote sensing big data: Management and applications. *Journal of Integrative Agriculture*, 17(9), 1915–1931.

Kerle, N., Janssen, L. L., & Huurneman, G. C. (2004). Principles of remote sensing. *ITC, Educational Textbook Series, 2*, 250.

Langhammer, J., Janský, B., Kocum, J., & Minaˇrík, R. (2018). 3-D reconstruction of an abandoned montane reservoir using UAV photogrammetry, aerial LiDAR and field survey. *Applied Geography, 98*, 9–21.

La Repubblica: Matese, A., & Di Gennaro, S. (2015). *La viticoltura di precisione*. https://media.fupress.com/files/pdf/16/2385/5449.

Lecinski, J. (2011). *Winning the zero moment of truth*. Hoepli.

Lee, J., Suh, T., Roy, D., Baucus, M. (2019). Emerging Technology and Business Model Innovation: The Case of Artificial Intelligence. *Journal of Open Innovation: Technology, Market, and Complexity*.; 5(3):44.

Masini, M., Pasquini, J., & Segreto, G. (A cura di). (2017). *Marketing e comunicazione. Strategie, strumenti, casi pratici.* Hoepli.

Matese, A., & Di Gennaro, S. F. (2015). Technology in precision viticulture: A state of the art review. *International Journal of Wine Research, 7*, 69–81.

Matese, A., Toscano, P., Di Gennaro, S. F., Genesio, L., Vaccari, F. P., Primicerio, J., ... & Gioli, B. (2015). Intercomparison of UAV, aircraft and satellite remote sensing platforms for precision viticulture. *Remote Sensing, 7*(3), 2971–2990.

Mercuri, F. (2020). Le determinanti della R&S nei processi di Industria 4.0. In Quattrociocchi, B., & Boria, P. (A cura di), *Ricerca e sviluppo quali fattori di crescita e di promozione per le imprese.* Jovene Editore.

Moudrý, V., Gdulová, K., Fogl, M., Klápste, P., Urban, R., Komárek, J., Moudrá, L., Stroner, M., Barták, V., & Solský, M. (2019). Comparison of leaf-off and leaf-on combined UAV imagery and airborne LiDAR for assessment of a post-mining site terrain and vegetation structure: Prospects for monitoring hazards and restoration success. *Applied Geography, 104*, 32–41.

Murray, C. C., & Chu, A. G. (2015). The flying sidekick traveling salesman problem: Optimization of drone-assisted parcel delivery. *Transportation Research Part C, 54*, 86–109.

Na, S., Park, C., So, K., Park, J., & Lee, K. (2017). Mapping the spatial distribution of barley growth based on unmanned aerial vehicle. In *6th International Conference on Agro-Geoinformatics* (pp. 1–5). IEEE Publications.

Negri, E., Fumagalli, L., & Macchi, M. (2017). A review of the roles of digital twin in CPS-based production systems. *Procedia Manufacturing, 11,* 939–948.

Pastore, A., & Vernuccio, M. (2016). *Impresa e comunicazione. Principi e strumenti per il management.* Apogeo Edizioni.

Pedrazzini, A. (2018, July 3). *L'industria 4.0 è un'occasione per valorizzare persone e competenze.* Il Sole 24 Ore.

Pepe, M., Fregonese, L., & Scaioni, M. (2018). Planning airborne photogrammetry and remote-sensing missions with modern platforms and sensors. *European Journal of Remote Sensing, 51*(1), 412–436.

Piccarreta, F., & Ceraudo, G. (2000). *Manuale di aerofotografi a archeologica. Metodologia, tecniche e applicazioni.* Edipuglia.

Pierce, F. J., & Nowak, P. (1999). Aspects of precision agriculture. In *Advances in agronomy* (Vol. 67, pp. 1–85). Academic Press.

Pirnie, B. R., Vick, A., Grissom, A., Mueller, K. P., & Orletsky, D. T. (2005). *Beyond close air support: Forging a new air-ground partnership* [Technical report]. RAND Corporation Santa Monica.

Poggiani, A., & Pratesi, C. (2016). *Marketing digitale.* McGraw-Hill Education.

Poropat, G. V. (1993). Effect of system point spread function, apparent size, and detector instantaneous field of view on the infrared image contrast of small objects. *Optical Engineering, 32*(10), 2598–2607.

Quattrociocchi, B. (2020). Competitività, IoT e Bonus ricercar e sviluppo. In Quattrociocchi, B., & Boria, P. (A cura di), *Ricerca e sviluppo quali fattori di crescita e di promozione per le imprese.* Jovene Editore.

Reim, W., Åström, J., & Eriksson, O. (2020). Implementation of Artificial Intelligence (AI): A Roadmap for Business Model Innovation. *AI, 1*(2), 180–191. doi:10.3390/ai1020011.

Yan, R. J., Pang, S., Sun, H. B., & Pang, Y. J. (2010). Development and missions of unmanned surface vehicle. *Journal of Marine Science and Application, 9*(4), 451–457.

Reddy, L. B., & DeLaurentis, D. (2016). Opinion survey to reduce uncertainty in public and stakeholder perception of unmanned aircraft. *Transportation Research Record, 2600,* 80–93.

Rees, W. G. (2013). *Physical principles of remote sensing.* Cambridge University Press.

Report Italia 4.0. (2018). www.deloitte.com.it.

Rick, J. W. (1996). Total stations in archaeology. *Society for American Archaeology Bulletin, 14*(4), 24–27.

Rodríguez, R. M., Alarcón, F., Rubio, D. S., & Ollero, A. (2013). Autonomous management of an UAV airfield. In *Proceedings of the 3rd International Conference on Application and Theory of Automation in Command and Control Systems,* Naples, Italy, 28–30 May.

Russell, M. T. (2016). *Fire chief perception of unmanned aircraft systems: A diffusion study.* Dissertation City University.

Short, N. M. (2003). A remote sensing tutorial. *Online Journal of Space Communication, 2*(3), 2.

Simone, C., Barile, S., & Grandinetti, R. (2021). The emergence of new market spaces: Brokerage and firm cognitive endowment. *Journal of Business Research, 134,* 457–466.

Snow, C. (2019). Amazon's drone delivery plans: What's old, what's new and when? https://www.forbes.com/sites/colinsnow/2019/06/17 /amazons-drone-delivery-whats-old-whats-new-and-when/ #6a2eadbf35f9.

Solodov, A., Williams, A., Al Hanaei, S., & Goddard, B. (2018). Analyzing the threat of unmanned aerial vehicles (UAV) to nuclear facilities. *Security Journal, 31*(1), 305–324.

Tam, A. (2011). *Public perception of unmanned air vehicles,* paper 3. Aviation Technology Graduate Student Publications.

Timmers, P. (1998). Business models for electronic markets. *Journal of Electronic Markets, 8,* 3–8. http://dx.doi.org/10.1080/101967898 00000016.

Toth, C., & Józków, G. (2016). Remote sensing platforms and sensors: A survey. *ISPRS Journal of Photogrammetry and Remote Sensing, 115,* 22–36.

Van Der Aalst, W. M. P., Burattin, A., De Leoni, M., Guzzo, A., Maggi F. M., & Montali, M. (2012). Process mining: Come estrarre conoscenza dai log dei sistemi informativi orientati ai processi. *Mondo Digitale,* 1–2.

Wang, Z., & Sheu, J.-B. (2019). Vehicle routing problem with drones. *Transportation Research. Part B, Methodological, 122*, 350–364.

Weiss, M., Jacob, F., & Duveiller, G. (2020). Remote sensing for agricultural applications: A meta-review. *Remote Sensing of Environment, 236*, 111402.

West, J. P., & Bowman, J. S. (2016). The domestic use of drones: An ethical analysis of surveillance issues. *Public Administration Review, 76*(4), 649–659.

Xu, G., Liu, Q., Chen, L., & Liu, L. (2016). Remote sensing for China's sustainable development: Opportunities and challenges. *Journal of Remote Sensing, 20*(5), 679–688.

Zink, M., & Bamler, R. (1995). X-SAR radiometric calibration and data quality. *IEEE Transactions on Geoscience and Remote Sensing, 33*(4), 840–847.

Index

www.ingramcontent.com/pod-product-compliance
Ingram Content Group UK Ltd.
Pitfield, Milton Keynes, MK11 3LW, UK
UKHW020417010325
455677UK00029B/930